FOSSILS

NEW
HOLLAND

This edition published in 2013 by New Holland Publishers
First published in 2007 by New Holland Publishers (UK) Ltd.
London • Cape Town • Sydney • Auckland
www.newhollandpublishers.com

Garfield House, 86–88 Edgware Road, London W2 2EA, UK
Unit 1, 66 Gibbes Street, Chatswood, NSW 2067, Australia
Wembley Square, First Floor, Solan Road Gardens, Cape Town, 8001, South Africa
218 Lake Road, Northcote, Auckland, New Zealand

10 9 8 7 6 5 4 3 2 1

ISBN 978 1 78009 408 3

Senior Editor: Sally McFall
Designer: Lorena Susak
Production: Olga Dementiev
Publisher: Simon Papps

Printed and bound in China by Toppan Leefung Printing Ltd

Pictures appearing on the cover:

Front cover: top, left to right: *Quenstedtoceras; Glossopteris; Lonsdaleia;* bottom: *Williamsonia,
Alethopteris, Gingko.*
Back cover: Amber with gnat

FOSSILS

A PHOTOGRAPHIC FIELD GUIDE

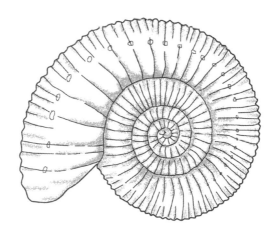

Chris and Helen Pellant

CONTENTS

INTRODUCTION

What are fossils?

Although we may take the fossilized remains of plants and animals for granted, it is remarkable to realize that the traces and remains of past organisms have been locked away in the rocks of the Earth's crust for many millions of years.

Literally, a fossil is 'something dug up', and the definition of what constitutes a fossil must be broad for it to be of any scientific use. It has to cover the traces of primitive algae found in rocks over 1,000 million years old; the shells of Jurassic molluscs changed into silica; the black carbon impression of a delicate fern leaf in mudstone from the coal bearing rocks of the Carboniferous period; the virtually complete insect trapped in Baltic amber of Cenozoic age, and the footprints left by a dinosaur running across wet Cretaceous mud. 'Any trace of past life preserved in the rocks of the Earth's crust' is a good working definition of a fossil. There is some overlap with archaeology in the very youngest layers of sediment. Items such as coins and human artefacts are generally not regarded as fossils, but the province of the archaeologist.

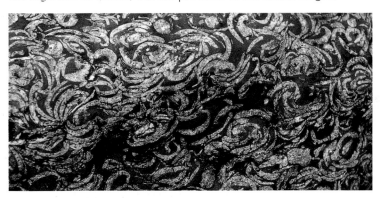

ABOVE: Mass of bivalve shells in ironstone. This fossilized shell bank has been cut through by erosion to reveal a cross-section of each shell.
*OPPOSITE: Ammonite **Quenstedtoceras**. The shimmering original shell is preserved on these ammonites.*

The branch of geology that deals with fossils is called palaeontology. Some palaeontologists study past habitats to see how communities of organisms lived and changed, while others use fossils to correlate strata from place to place and work out the sequence of the rocks. Our evidence for evolution is in the fossil record, and the research of some palaeontologists focuses on this.

It is very important to remember that fossils are biological material, even if their chemical composition may have been changed. Palaeontology is in many ways a study of the natural history of the past. The names given to fossils have thus to follow the rules set out for biological naming, and the classification of fossils must abide by the same principles. Immediately there can be problems. A biological species is defined relatively easily. It can replicate itself, and a study of its genetics will help define the limits of any species.

Fossils are the long dead remains of organisms, often only fragments of the animal or plant, so fossil species can be difficult to determine. In the past, the variation that can occur within a species has often not been taken into account. These variations within any species may be caused by genetic and environmental influences. Also, changes take place during ontogeny. This is the development of an individual from birth to death. Many animals (arthropods, for example) moult as they develop and grow, and vertebrate skeletons may change considerably during the animal's life. So, fossils of juveniles can be found that do not resemble the adults of the species. As long as a large number of fossils thought to be of one species are studied, to allow for variations of the types mentioned, a fossil species can be established.

ABOVE: Insects in amber. Fossils can be perfectly preserved organisms, such as these entire specimens.

How fossils are formed

Only a very small fraction of all the organisms that have lived is preserved in the fossil record. When a plant or animal dies, it may decompose, be eaten by scavengers, or fragmented by erosion. Unless it is buried by sediment, it stands little chance of becoming a fossil. Land creatures are less likely to be buried in this way than creatures that live in the sea, where sediment accumulates on the seabed and eventually can be changed into rock. It also helps considerably if the organism has some hard parts. These are more likely to survive at least for some time before burial by sediment takes place.

Taphonomy is the study of the changes that occur between an organism's dying and its becoming a fossil. In order for a fossil to form, the remains of an organism must be in chemical balance with its surroundings. As sediments turn into sedimentary rocks, many changes can take place. These are called diagenesis, and include

ABOVE: **Aptyxiella.** *These gastropod shells have been dissolved, leaving their impression on the surrounding rock. In some, there are internal casts.*

chemical and physical changes. The calcite (calcium carbonate) of which a mollusc shell is largely composed may not survive profound changes in the sediment in which the shell was originally buried.

Fossils may be simple casts made of mud or sand that filled in a hollow in the sediment where a shell or dinosaur's foot had been pressed down. In this case there is nothing left of the actual organism. A similar type of fossil can form when shells buried in rock strata are dissolved, leaving a hollow. Minerals seeping through the rock may, at a later time, fill these gaps and create a replica of the shell.

Other fossils are made of material very different from the original shell or bone. In some rock environments a chemical replacement takes place. The molecules of calcite of which a mollusc shell, or coral, is composed can be replaced by a new mineral that is stable deep underground. In this way, perfect replicas of the organism

ABOVE: **Laevitrigonia.** *The shell of this bivalve mollusc has dissolved to leave an internal cast, which shows details such as the hinge teeth and muscle scars.*

are made that can survive their new environment. Shells may be replaced by pyrite, quartz, hematite or other minerals. This is the process called 'petrifaction'.

Many plant fossils are delicate, black, carbon-rich patterns on rock surfaces. Carbon is an essential element in all living things, and during the fossilization of leaves, often only the carbon is left. Plant fossils can also form when hollow stems and tree trunks are filled in with sediment such as river sand, preserving the fossil in three dimensions. The Rhynie chert, found in the Grampian region of Scotland, UK, is famous for the preservation of plant tissue in three dimensions by replacement with silica.

Exceptionally detailed fossils can be created when organisms are buried in very fine-grained sediment. The limestones at Solnhofen, in Germany, and the Burgess shales in British Columbia, Canada, are two well-documented examples. At Solnhofen, even the impressions of feathers are preserved, and the Burgess shale

ABOVE: *The calcium carbonate of this Carboniferous coral has been replaced by hematite (iron oxide). The septa are clearly visible.*

contains fossils of all manner of strange, soft-bodied creatures that lived in the Cambrian sea.

There are many instances of the original organic material being retained, and of the perfect preservation of delicate structures. For example, insects have been trapped in resin seeping from pine trees, which later turned into amber and perfectly preserved them. Larger animals have been virtually entirely fossilized in frozen ground of the tundra or in naturally seeping tar pits. Examples of these are explained at relevant points in the book.

ABOVE: Opal tree. Opal, which is a semi-precious form of silica, has replaced the original tissue of this tree trunk. Faint outlines of the growth rings can be seen.

OPPOSITE: Quartz ammonite shell. When broken, the internal chambers in an ammonite shell are visible. This specimen, replaced with quartz, has small crystals in the chambers.

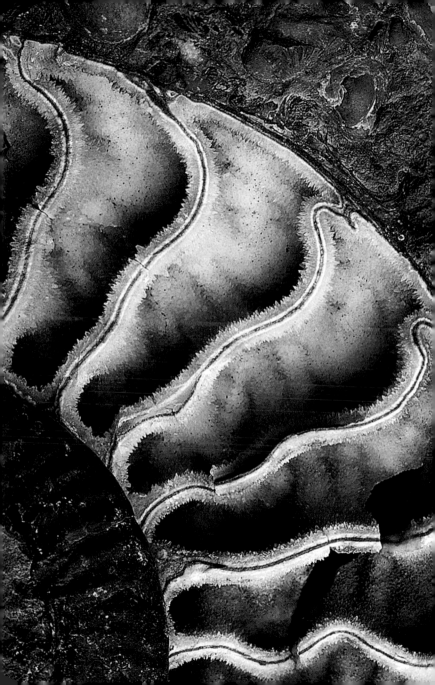

Naming and classifying fossils

Because fossils are biological material, they have to be named according to the rules that biologists use. These rules were established in the 18th century by Carolus Linnaeus, a Swedish naturalist. When he was cataloguing plants and animals, he found that there were many different names in various languages for each organism. He chose Latin as the language for his new naming system. The system he pioneered is still universally used today. Each species is given a two-word name. The first word is the generic name and the second the specific name. In some cases three words are used, and if so, the third word is the sub-species name. These should be written in italics, with a capital letter for the generic name. To be able to identify a fossil to its generic level is a good standard, and the fossils illustrated in this book are given their generic names.

The classification of animals and plants consists of groupings of similar organisms, with very broad groups being subdivided until the species level is reached. It may be helpful to classify a fossil in order to show how the system works. One of the commonest and best-known ammonite species is *Dactylioceras commune* (p.178), *Dactylioceras* being the name of the **genus** and *commune* that of the **species**. It occurs in marine, Lower Jurassic, sedimentary rocks in many parts of the world. There are a number of ammonites that resemble this species but show enough variation to be regarded as different species, though they are members of the same genus. *Dactylioceras tenuicostatum* is a further species within the same genus, which is used as a zone fossil in the Lower Jurassic. These ammonites and many others are grouped in the **family** Eoderocerataceae, and, along with the other ammonite families, they are placed in the **order** Ammonitida. Ammonites are closely related to squids and octopods, and all these are in the **class** Cephalopoda. As the grouping continues to widen and encompasses more and more creatures, ammonites are placed in the **phylum** Mollusca, along with organisms such as the nautilus, clams and snails. Beyond this category, we reach the **kingdom** Animalia.

If you can't identify and name a fossil you have found, take it to a local museum or university geology department. There will be experts there to help you in identifying any fossil you have found.

Always make a note of where you find specimens, as this will be of great help in identification.

ABOVE: These two ammonites are placed in the same genus, as they are very similar and lived at the same time in the early Jurassic. However, because of subtle differences, they are given different specific names. **D. tenuicostatum** *(left) has finer ribs compared with the thicker ribbed* **D. commune** *(right). The Latin* **'tenuicostatum'** *means 'slender ribbed', and the Latin* **'commune'** *means 'common'. The specimen of* **D. commune** *has been carved with a snake-like head to perpetuate the myth that these fossils were snakes turned to stone.*

Uses of fossils

There are a number of ways in which fossils are useful to geologists in helping them to understand the history of the Earth and to determine what the environment was like in any given place at different times during the past.

The study of past environments and the use of fossils to show how conditions have changed is called palaeoecology. One of the guiding principles of geology, which can well be applied to palaeoecological investigations, was originally proposed by Sir Charles Lyell, who was born in Angus, Scotland, UK, and educated at the University of Oxford. His book, *Principles of Geology*, published between 1830 and 1833, included the idea of uniformitarianism. This principle suggested that the geological events we see happening in and on the Earth's crust today have been taking place throughout geological time, and so rocks and past events can be interpreted in terms of current phenomena. The phrase 'the present is the key to the past' is a fair summary of what

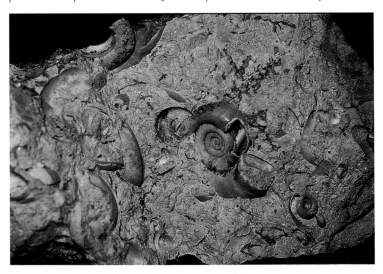

ABOVE: Freshwater limestone. Recent forms of the gastropod **Planorbis** *live in fresh water. The same genus is fossilized in this limestone, and it can be assumed that the rock was formed in similar conditions.*

uniformitarianism is about. This generally works very well, but the further we are removed from our reference point, which is the Earth today, the less we may be able to apply this principle. The young Earth was much hotter internally than it is now, and the chemistry of the oceans and the early atmosphere was very different: for example, before the proliferation of green plants, there was virtually no oxygen in the air.

Back into the Palaeozoic and Mesozoic eras, sensible palaeogeographic reconstructions can be made, usually by comparing fossils to their modern relatives. The vast majority of fossils are of marine organisms, so it is marine environments that tend to occupy palaeontologists most. On a broad level, it is easy to tell that rocks were formed on the seabed if they contain fossil corals, brachiopods, echinoderms and certain molluscs. However, by looking in detail at the fossils and their associations, it is possible to see how environments change. For example, the corals found fossilized in Lower Carboniferous rocks in North America and Europe are very similar in many respects to those found today building reefs in tropical seas. It is thus reasonable to propose that warm, shallow seas covered these areas at the time the corals lived there. An example of a very detailed reconstruction of conditions is that of the Purbeck beds of Southern England. These span the Jurassic/Cretaceous boundary, and are a varied group of shales and thin limestones, which were deposited in lagoons and lakes near the open sea. Some strata here contain fossil ostracods (small bivalved arthropods) and algae that could withstand hypersaline conditions. These rocks were probably formed when evaporation of a lagoon had increased the salt content of the water. The bivalve mollusc *Unio* and the gastropod *Viviparus*, fossilized in other strata, imply that seawater had flooded the area and brackish conditions were established. In some rocks at Purbeck, fossil oysters and the echinoid *Hemicidaris* occur. These indicate fully marine conditions. Very shallow-water or even land-formed sediments are suggested by dinosaur footprints found on some bedding planes.

Stratigraphy is the branch of geology that places the rocks in sequence, with the oldest first, and also correlates strata from place to place. Ever since the early years of the 19th century, the use of fossils for this work has been recognized. William Smith, an English canal engineer, showed in his *Strata Identified by Organised Fossils* (1816) how rocks in one locality could be equated to strata some distance away by using their contained fossils. However, only certain fossils can be used with precision for stratigraphic work. These are called zone fossils, and small parts of geological time are named after them. A zone fossil needs to have lived for only a short time. It thus tends to have a relatively short vertical range within strata. In order for it to be useful in correlating rocks from place to place, it should have a wide geographical distribution; free-swimming marine organisms are ideal. Fossils that are common and easily recognized, and have a hard shell, are better than rare ones, or those that are soft bodied. The relative geological time scale has been divided into time zones using fossils such as graptolites and ammonites, but no absolute times can be determined using fossils. Absolute time is calculated using radiometric dating.

Fossils are our key to the understanding of evolution and how it can be driven by mutation and extinction. Some fossils are found in strata of widely differing ages and seem to have lived as a genus for many millions of years. Others apparently lived for only a short period of time before being replaced in a certain habitat by another genus. When large numbers of fossils of a particular species are collected for analysis, it is often found that there are typical forms and also some individuals that are larger, smaller or different in some other way. These different individuals may have features that allow them to survive better in certain environments, and even develop into new species. A careful study of a group of fossils through progressively younger strata will show how species evolve and change with time. At certain points there are sudden radiations with the rapid evolution of many species. This happened, for example, early in the Cambrian period, possibly because for the first time oxygen was seeping into the air and oceans in reasonable quantity. The evolution of life and the fossil record are punctuated by numerous extinctions. The mass extinction at the end of the Cretaceous period is well documented, as it was at this time that the dinosaurs finally died out, as did the vast majority of marine invertebrates, including the ammonites. In the Cenozoic period, the fossil record changes, and mammals became dominant on land, having survived the Cretaceous extinction.

OPPOSITE: **Didymograptus**. *Graptolites make good zone fossils. They were carried great distances by ocean currents, and are common in Palaeozoic deep-water sedimentary rocks.*

The rocks that contain fossils

Geologists classify rocks into three main groups, igneous rocks, sedimentary rocks and metamorphic rocks. Igneous rocks result from the consolidation of lava on the Earth's surface, or of magma deep underground. Metamorphic rocks have undergone profound changes brought about by heat, pressure or a combination of both. Neither of these two types of rocks generally contains fossils. However, volcanic ash and dust can settle in water and preserve marine organisms, and the least altered metamorphic rocks, including slate, may contain rather distorted fossils that occurred in the pre-metamorphosed rocks. Sedimentary rocks form on the Earth's crust and are the ones that contain most fossils.

Because of the way they are deposited as mud, sand or other material, sedimentary rocks have a characteristic feature called stratification or bedding. Each stratum represents the deposition of sediment on the seabed, in a lake or river, or possibly on the land surface, and these strata generally make sedimentary rocks easy to distinguish from the two other main types, though some metamorphic rocks, such as slate, have a 'layered' appearance produced by cleavage (parallel surfaces in a fine-grained metamorphic rock, caused by mineral alignment).

There are different types of sedimentary rock, and in order to understand their formation and origins, they are organised into three main groups. Sandstones and similar rocks are classified as detrital or fragmentary sediments. Conglomerates, breccias, mudstones and shales as well as sandstones are in this group. These rocks are all made of materials, like sand grains or clay particles, that have been eroded and weathered from pre-formed rocks, and then carried by rivers and deposited, often in the sea. Many different fossils are found in these rocks, depending on their age and the environment of deposition. Land-formed sandstones and shales may have plant fossils and the remains of vertebrates. Marine shales and clays are often rich in arthropod and mollusc fossils. Fine-grained rocks like these can preserve great detail.

Organic sedimentary rocks, as the name suggests, are composed of material derived from plants and animals. Perfect fossils can

RIGHT: Sedimentary rocks are easily recognized by stratification, or bedding. Here, red chalk underlies white chalk on the coast of Norfolk, UK.

be extracted from these rocks, though often they consist of fragmented material. Crinoidal and coral limestones are organic sediments, made from what were originally seabed banks of crinoid stems, or coral reefs inundated with lime-rich mud. There are many other examples of fossil-rich limestones full of gastropod shells and even ammonites. These rocks tend to be pale-coloured and may produce characteristic landscapes with little surface water because of their porosity or permeability.

Some sedimentary rocks are chemically formed. These include oolitic limestone, which is made of small grains called ooliths, composed of concentric layers of calcite precipitated around a minute shell fragment or sand grain. Ooliths are only a millimetre or two in diameter. Such rocks form today in shallow marine areas, and those from the past frequently contain many fossils of organisms such as corals, brachiopods, molluscs and echinoderms.

Searching for fossils
Good preparation, before looking for fossils, often ensures the best results. Some amazing specimens have been found by complete chance, but research is a sensible first step. Guide books and geological maps will indicate, often in detail, the best places to search. Geological maps may, at first sight, seem to be very complicated. They show the areas where different rocks occur at the surface, and also have cross sections showing the structure of those rocks below ground. However, many of the places on the map, coloured to indicate the outcrop of a certain rock type, will have towns and other obstructions on the ground. It is only where a rock is exposed that it can be seen and examined. By studying the map carefully, exposures can be discovered, for example where a certain stratum is cut by a river valley, or where it reaches the coast. Man-made exposures, such as road cuttings, are often excellent, as are excavations for new buildings and pipelines. Permission should always be obtained before going onto private land, and care should be taken near safety hazards such as cliff faces, from which rocks may fall.

Collecting in the field should always be done in moderation, and a geological hammer used only for breaking up loose rocks rather than for quarrying at a rock face. It is essential to care for any specimens found as soon as they are collected. They should be placed in collecting bags and material such as 'bubble wrap' used to protect them. Details of each specimen, including the location and date found, should be entered in a notebook, and a sketch of the location may also help to identify material. The scientific importance of any specimen is enhanced if its exact location is documented.

Collected fossils must be cleaned, identified and housed safely. Most specimens will have rock and mud adhering to them. It may damage a fossil to remove much of the rock matrix, but loose material can be removed with a toothbrush or paintbrush. Small screwdrivers, knife blades and other everyday tools may be helpful. Distilled water can be used to wash specimens, but care should be taken if using other cleaning liquids. Dilute hydrochloric acid will remove limestone, but will also destroy any fossils made of calcium carbonate. The best specimens can be displayed, but if left in the open they will collect dust, so it is best to place them in glass cases. For the bulk of a collection, strong metal or wooden cabinets are ideal, but the individual specimens should be prevented from rubbing against each other

ABOVE: This Sigillaria *fossil shows the base of the entire stem of a giant lycopod plant, along with part of its root structure.*

Geological time-scale

The Geological Time-scale: Explanations

Geologists look at time in two different ways. There is relative time, subdivided using fossils, and absolute time, which is determined by radiometric dating.

The rocks in the Earth's crust have been ordered into a **relative time-scale**, so that they can be understood in sequence and studied in manageable units. The divisions between the periods have been chosen by considering major geological events and changes in the fossil record. Often an unconformity or other significant change in the strata marks the boundary between different eras and different periods. An unconformity represents a gap in the geological record. The deposition of strata is a record of geological time, as each stratum takes time to accumulate. Where there is an unconformity, strata may have been folded and eroded and then new rocks deposited, or there may have been a break in deposition. The erosion surface or other break marks the unconformity; we can only guess at what events may have taken place during the unrecorded time.

The time-scale used today was established, at least in outline, by pioneering geologists working in the 19th century, and many of the names for the main eras and periods go back to those days. These names come from various sources, and many of them are from the UK. The words used for the eras mean ancient, middle and recent life, but some of the names of the periods may be obscure. Cambrian is named after Wales, where early research into rocks of that age was undertaken. Ordovician and Silurian were named after ancient tribes who inhabited Wales and the Welsh border country. Devonian rocks were originally studied in Devon, and the Carboniferous system contains the richest deposits of coal, a carbon-rich fuel. The Permian rocks are named after a province in Russia, while the Triassic period is subdivided into three parts at its type locality in Germany. The Jura Mountains in France give their name to the Jurassic period, and the Cretaceous rocks are so called after the Greek word for chalk, 'creta'. The words 'era' and 'period' refer to units of geological time. The term 'system' is used for the rocks formed

LEFT: Alternating Lower Jurassic shale and limestone strata in Somerset, UK.

at a particular time. So, for example, rocks of the Jurassic system were formed during the Jurassic period.

The word 'Pre-Cambrian' at the base of any geological time-scale usually has the status of neither an era nor a period, as it is such a large piece of time. On the basis of radiometric dating and stratigraphy, it has been subdivided. In 2004, the Neoproterozoic era, at the very end of Pre-Cambrian time, was established, containing the Ediacaran period. Palaeontology was one of the main reasons for this refinement of the time-scale. The well-known Ediacaran fossil assemblage of algae and other primitive organisms is named after the Ediacaran Hills of South Australia. Similar organisms are found in Russia, Namibia and central England.

Absolute time is denoted by actual numbers and the letters **Ma** (millions of years ago). To work out the ages of rocks is theoretically simple, but the science involves complex calculations and precise measurements at an atomic level. When certain rocks are formed, their minerals contain small amounts of radioactivity. For example, feldspar, a very common mineral in granite, can contain radioactive potassium. Rubidium, another radioactive element, is also found in igneous rocks. Because they are radioactive, these elements decay spontaneously into other more stable material, called daughter elements. The rate of decay can be accurately calculated. If the amount of daughter element in a rock is measured and the rate of decay is known, then it is possible to say for how long the change has been taking place: the time since the radioactive element was trapped in the rock is the age of that rock. However, there are problems with this method. For example, the decay product of potassium is argon, a gas, which may leak from rocks, and so measurements may give a low figure for argon actually trapped in the rock. This may suggest that the decay has been taking place for less time than it actually has, resulting in an underestimation of the age. Furthermore, radiometric dating techniques can only be applied to certain rocks. Igneous and some metamorphic rocks are ideal, because they crystallize at a fairly definite time, trapping radioactive elements. Most sedimentary rocks are not much use for this dating technique, as they do not contain the right minerals and are often the products of weathering and erosion, thus containing materials from older rocks. Radiometric dating results, together with the relative time-scale and when seen in the context of other calculated ages, provide an accurate time-scale.

Geological Time Scale

ERA	PERIOD	EPOCH	AGE (MA)
		HOLOCENE (RECENT)	FROM 0.01
	NEOGENE	PLEISTOCENE	1.8–0.01
		PLIOCENE	5.3–1.8
CENOZOIC		MIOCENE	23–5.3
		OLIGOCENE	34–23
	PALAEO-GENE	EOCENE	56–34
		PALAEOCENE	65–56
	CRETACEOUS		142–65
MESOZOIC	JURASSIC		206–142
	TRIASSIC		248–206
	PERMIAN		290–248
	CARBONIF-EROUS		354–290
PALAEOZOIC	DEVONIAN		417–354
	SILURIAN		443–417
	ORDOVICIAN		495–443
	CAMBRIAN		545–495
PRE-CAMBRIAN			4,500–545

FOSSIL PLANTS

Because much plant tissue, especially that of leaves and flowers, is delicate, and because many plants live on land, their fossil remains are uncommon. Plant fossils are often black carbon films on bedding surfaces, the carbon being all that remains of the original plant tissue. In some extreme cases, as at Mazon Creek, Illinois, in the USA (see page36), three-dimensional leaf fossils have been preserved. The stems of large plants, often filled with sediment or replaced with silicon dioxide (quartz or opal), make good fossils, as do resistant pollen grains, though these need microscope examination in order to study and identify them. On land there is much erosion and weathering, so even if land plant remains are covered with sediment, this may easily be removed. Plants often break up when they die. The roots, leaves and stem may become fossilized in different places, and in some cases these different parts of the same plant have been given different biological names.

The earliest plant fossils are the remains of algae preserved in rocks of Pre-Cambrian age. These stromatolites (see page 32) are important because they released the first oxygen into the Earth's primitive atmosphere. The early Earth was a colourless place, without the bright plant colours we take for granted today. In the Silurian period, simple vascular plants evolved, but it was not until the Devonian period that green became a common colour on the land. Our vast deposits of coal, which drove the industrial revolution of the 19th century and are still vital in power generation today, formed from the great forests of the Carboniferous period. True flowers appear relatively late in the fossil record, during late Mesozoic times. They have great significance in two ways: cross-pollination between flowers provides a way in which different combinations of genes can occur; pollen and nectar are the food for insects, which were then able to evolve rapidly. Plants very like those that grow today developed during the Cenozoic era.

Fossil plants are very useful in palaeogeographic reconstruction. Many plants are specialized in where they live, especially in terms of climate. By comparing fossil plants to modern genera, it is

LEFT: **Williamsonia.** *A common plant in the Jurassic period; the specimen shown here, much enlarged, is from North Yorkshire, UK.*

FOSSIL PLANTS

possible to suggest what climatic conditions existed in the past. The most detailed study of climate change using plant fossils has been carried out on fossil pollen from glacial and post-glacial deposits. Pollen is very resistant material, and each plant can be recognized by its own distinctive pollen grains. These can be obtained from peat and other deposits and studied microscopically. Certain species disappeared in sequence with the onset of cold conditions and reappeared as the climate ameliorated during interglacials and in the current post-glacial.

SOLENOPORA (I)

This fossil is made up of slender porous tubes that were secreted by an alga. They are calcareous and branching, often with a Y-shaped structure. Algae such as these are frequently found in reefs of sediment. Along with other fossils such as bryozoans, they help to bind fine-grained sediment together and allow reefs to build up.

Size: The tubes are very small, the field of view being about 50mm (2in).
Occurrence: This type of *Solenopora* is found worldwide in rocks ranging in age from Ordovician to Jurassic. The specimen shown above is from the Ordovician of southern Norway.

Comments: Two forms of this alga are illustrated (see also below). They have very different structures, one composed of small branching tubes, the other a banded mound of calcium carbonate. Algae of this type have an important role in food chains, providing food and shelter for many other marine organisms. Also, they live in relatively shallow water and use sunlight for photosynthesis, giving off oxygen. Many algae leave no trace, as their tissues are not readily fossilized, but some secrete structures made of calcium carbonate, as shown in the illustrations.

SOLENOPORA (II)

Size: The illustrated specimen (below) is 120mm (4⅘in) long.
Occurrence: *Solenopora* is found in strata ranging in age from Lower Palaeozoic to Recent, worldwide. The specimen shown is of Jurassic age from Gloucestershire, UK.
Comments: *Solenopora jurassica* has a different form from the tube-shaped example from Norway (see opposite left). It is made of alternating pink and white bands of calcium carbonate, and grew as a mound-shaped structure on the Jurassic seabed. Close examination of the layering shows that the colours may be linked to changes in the nature of the algal deposit. Porous layers alternate

FOSSIL PLANTS

with bands of lower porosity. It has been suggested that pigmented material was concentrated in the less porous layers by downward moving water. This may have occurred after formation. Because of its colouring, it is known as 'beetroot stone'.

STROMATOLITES

Stromatolites are layered mounds of calcareous material secreted by blue-green algae. They are forming in relatively few areas today, but these include Western Australia, where stromatolites flourish in highly saline water, which is often too salty for other organisms. The mounds grow in very shallow conditions, with their tops above sea level at certain times.

Fossil stromatolites are among the oldest remains of living organisms, and some have been dated at over 3,500 million years. They were abundant during Pre-Cambrian times and had a profound effect on the Earth's early environment. Blue-green algae, the organisms that build stromatolites, produce oxygen;

OPPOSITE TOP: An example from Jurassic strata, showing in close-up the curved layers. Each mound measures 100mm (4in) across.
OPPOSITE BELOW: This example is from Ordovician strata on the north coast of Scotland. The mounds measure 500mm (20in) across.

with their development, this gas, which was not present in the Earth's primitive atmosphere, became significant. Initially the oxygen was used to convert iron into minerals (iron compounds) such as hematite (iron oxide). Some of the very rich banded ironstone deposits mined today date from these times. Gradually, as the oxygen produced was not entirely taken up in compounds, some of it was released into the ocean and atmosphere. This vital gas became an important part of the atmosphere, and the blue-green algae and anaerobic bacteria which make stromatolite mounds were restricted to very specialized habitats, where oxygen is lacking. The algae secrete a mat of lime, trapping sediment. As they grow through it, mounds are created.

COOKSONIA

The delicate plant remains seen here are of the first vascular plant known in the fossil record. Its stiff structure allowed the plant to stand up from the ground, and within its stems there are cells of water-transporting xylem. Slender roots anchored the plant, but it was leafless. It reproduced in much the same way as modern ferns.
Size: Field of view of specimen is 70mm (2⅘in) across.
Occurrence: *Cooksonia* has been found in Europe, North America,

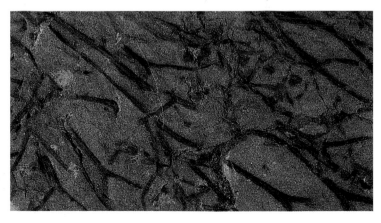

Antarctica, Africa and Asia. The specimen is from rocks of Devonian age in Orkney, Scotland, UK.

Comments: Spores from *Cooksonia* have been discovered in rocks of Devonian age in Shropshire, UK. As they developed, each would have produced a prothallus, a small, green structure containing both male and female reproductive organs. If many spores developed in a small area, the ground would become green with the prothalli.

PARKA

Another very early plant adapted to living on land, *Parka* consisted of a rounded thallus, here seen to be composed of many small, round structures. Like *Cooksonia*, *Parka* reproduced with spores. These were coated with strong cuticle to allow them to survive before they germinated.

Size: Specimen shown 30mm (1⅛in) in diameter.
Occurrence: Worldwide in rocks of Silurian and Devonian age.

The specimen illustrated here is from Devonian rocks in Angus, Scotland, UK.

NEUROPTERIS

Neuropteris is a well-known genus of pteridosperm (seed fern) often found in coal-bearing strata of Carboniferous age. It is a non-flowering, fern-like plant, the leaves composed of a number of small leaflets. The line running down each leaflet, the mid-rib, has

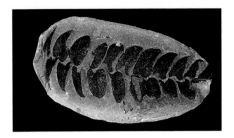

numerous small, curved veins running from it. The leaves of this genus are usually found isolated from the main plant.

Size: The specimen is 50mm (2in) long.

Occurrence: From Carboniferous strata in North America and Europe. The specimen is from Lancashire, UK.

Comments: Seed ferns are only known from the fossil record and they were common through out the Upper Palaeozoic. Because they are similar in structure to ferns, they were originally grouped with them. Research has shown significant differences, and they are now in a separate group – pteridosperms.

EUPECOPTERIS

This specimen shows typical Mazon Creek preservation in an iron-rich nodule. These nodules contain much siderite (iron carbonate), and plant material is preserved three-dimensionally, rather than as a one-dimensional film of carbon. *Eupecopteris* is a member of the pteridosperm group (seed ferns). The leaf seen here has the characteristic central midrib and many lateral leaflets.

Size: The specimen is 60mm (2⅖ in) long.

Occurrence: In Upper Carboniferous rocks in North America, Europe and Asia.

MAZON CREEK

The preservation of delicate plant tissues and the soft parts of animals is unusual in the fossil record. However, at Mazon Creek both occur. Coal strip-mining has for many years been carried out in Illinois, USA. The Pennsylvanian (Upper Carboniferous) coal-bearing rocks are overlain by shales containing ironstone nodules, in which amazing plant and animal fossils are found. It is probable that the nodules formed around the organisms soon after they were buried in sediment. Soft tissue is often preserved in great detail. There are two distinct sedimentary environments at Mazon Creek: marine and non-marine. The non-marine (both brackish and freshwater sediments) contain 350 land plant species and 140 species of insects. There are also centipedes, spiders, millipedes and scorpions, as well as amphibians, fish and crustaceans. The marine rocks have fish, including coelacanths and lampreys, worms, jellyfish and cephalopods. Surprisingly, the Mazon Creek fauna contains virtually none of the usual Carboniferous fossil assemblage, such as brachiopods, crinoids and molluscs. The creatures it does have are often unusual. For example, *Tullimonstrum*, which is only known from these rocks, is a segmented, soft-bodied animal which may belong to an extinct group. Many of the plant fossils are found elsewhere, but their preservation at Mazon Creek is usually exceptional.

ANNULARIA

This plant is classified with the Equisetales, or horsetails, a group well known today. *Annularia* grew with the leaves in whorls around the stem and branches coming from nodes. The leaves are delicate and flat, usually being slender with rounded tips, and are fused together at the point where they meet the stem.

Size: The leaf whorls can be up to 50mm (2in) across.

Occurrence: *Annularia* is found in strata of Upper Carboniferous and Permian age worldwide, and is very common in Carboniferous coal-bearing strata.

Comments: *Annularia* bore cones that are usually found as separate fossils, not joined to the main plant. Some horsetails, such as *Calamites* (p.42), are best known from their fossil stems, but it is the leaf whorls of *Annularia* that are common as fossils.

ALETHOPTERIS

This seed fern is commonly found in coal-bearing strata of Carboniferous age. *Alethopteris* has pinnate (compound) fronds. The leaflets have a broad base where they are attached. There are complex veins in the leaflets, some having a pronounced fork-shaped pattern. When compared with *Neuropteris* (pp.34–35) it is seen that the leaves of *Alethopteris* are more triangular in shape (see image on the opposite page).

Size: The specimen shown is 50mm (2in) long.

Occurrence: This genus is found in Upper Carboniferous and Permian rocks in North America and Europe. The specimen shown is from Kansas, USA.

LEPIDODENDRON

This is part of the stem of a lycopod, a giant clubmoss that grew to over 30m (100ft) in height. The marks on the specimen are leaf scars with a typical diamond-shaped pattern. Over a hundred species of this genus have been described, often on the basis of the way the leaves were attached to the stem.

Size: Whole plants are known to be over 30m (100ft) tall. Roots over 10m (33ft) long have been recorded.

Occurrence: Upper Carboniferous to Lower Permian, in Europe, Russia, North Africa, China and Mongolia. The specimen is from Staffordshire, UK.

Comments: *Lepidodendron* is a very common plant in the Upper Carboniferous coal measures and must have been a major contributor to the peat accumulations that ultimately became coal. As one of the tallest trees, it would have formed the forest canopy. Because the plant tended to break up, various parts of it have been given different fossil names. For instance, the roots, reaching out horizontally from the base of the stem, are called *Stigmaria*.

SIGILLARIA

The fossil depicted is part of a branching structure from a giant lycopod closely related to *Lepidodendron*. It shows the typical pattern of rows of small, oval indentations. These markings are where the linear leaves were attached. The plant had leaves growing in clumps from the branches, unlike many modern plants.

Size: The whole plant could reach 30m (100ft) in height.

Occurrence: *Sigillaria* was one of the main coal-forming plants and is found in Upper Carboniferous strata. The genus as a whole occurs from the Lower Carboniferous to the Permian in North America and Europe.

Comments: This specimen is part of a branch preserved in reddish mudstone.

COAL FORMATION

The plants of Upper Carboniferous age which are illustrated are among those which formed the great accumulations of coal. During this time a supercontinent called Gondwanaland existed, on which were vast forests and swamps. The climate varied from warm-temperate to sub-tropical, and much rainfall helped vegetation flourish. Peat accumulation in these forests was the basis of coal. There were great rivers running across the huge landmass, and where they reached the sea, deltas were built up from eroded sediment. Vegetation lived near sea level on the delta surface, and even small changes in sea level had a profound effect on these forests. When seawater flooded the delta top, the vegetation was killed off and buried beneath layers of sand and mud, becoming peat. These peat layers were thus interbedded with marine and deltaic sediments in sequences called cyclothems. When it is dried, peat will burn, and in many parts of the world it is used as a fuel, although it produces far less heat than coal. There are many changes which take place before peat becomes coal. Burial beneath layers of sediment increases not only pressure but also heat, and the volatiles in peat (mainly water) are gradually driven off. This increases the carbon percentage from the original 30% in peat to 40% in brown coal, or lignite. As lignite is further buried, bituminous coal (>75% carbon content) and anthracite (>80% carbon content) are produced. Coal is, in effect, a metamorphic rock, as it has been changed by heat and pressure from its original form.

CALAMITES

This plant belongs to the group called Equisetales, the horsetails. The stem, part of which is illustrated here, has longitudinal grooves. There are joints at right angles to these at regular intervals. Branches developed from nodes and the leaves grew from the stem in whorls. Inside the stem there was soft, pithy tissue that often decayed rapidly before fossilization. The fossil stems are thus often filled with sediment, or crushed on bedding planes, as in this example.
Size: The whole plant grew to about 30m (100ft).

Occurrence: A genus from Upper Carboniferous and Permian strata in North America, Europe, China, and South-East Asia. The specimen is from South Wales, UK.
Comments: Modern horsetails often inhabit marshy ground, and *Calamites* lived in abundance in the Upper Carboniferous swamp forests. Its plentiful remains helped to build up the peat deposits from which coal was formed.

SPHENOPTERIS

These are leaves from a shrubby type of pteridosperm (seed fern). Very little is known of the genus apart from its leaves, which can be recognised by their toothed edges. Like true ferns, these plants had fronds with an axis and pinnules. Rarely, fertile fronds bearing the reproductive bodies have been found as fossils.
Size: This specimen is 60mm (2⅜in) long.
Occurrence: From strata of Carboniferous and Permian age, worldwide.
Comments: *Sphenopteris* flourished in marshy conditions during

the Upper Carboniferous, and its delicate leaves are common fossils in the coal-bearing strata.

GLOSSOPTERIS

Glossopteris is a seed fern which may have grown with a tree-like habit, though some believe it to have been a bushy plant. Stems have been found with growth rings, but it is the leaves that are abundantly fossilized. These vary in shape, as shown by the two illustrations. The reddish-coloured specimens are narrow and long, the grey specimens (from Adamstown, Australia) are more oval in shape.
Size: The plant grew to 6m (19ft 6in) in height.
Occurrence: *Glossopteris* flourished on the supercontinent called Gondwanaland in the Permian and Triassic periods, and is found in Australia, Antarctica, South America, southern Africa, Madagascar, India and New Zealand.
Comments: This fossil plant has been of great value in the proof of continental drift.

FOSSIL PLANTS

CONIOPTERIS

Coniopteris is a true fern, and is similar to modern fern plants. The leaflets grow from a central stem, and each leaflet segment has indented margins.

Size: These fossils are about 20mm (⅘in) long.

Occurrence: A genus from strata of Mesozoic age from North America, Europe and Asia.

Comments: Here a group of leaves has been preserved as a film of carbon on a bedding plane of iron-rich sandstone.

WILLIAMSONIA

This genus belongs to the cycadophytes group, which is subdivided into the cycads and the Bennettitales. *Williamsonia* is within the

Bennettitales, all of which are extinct; they are characterized by a woody stem and rough, pinnate leaves.

Size: The specimen is about 25mm (1in) long. Whole plants may have been 2m (6ft, 6in) tall.

Occurrence: The Bennettitales range from Triassic to Upper Cretaceous, and *Williamsonia* is found in rocks of Jurassic age, worldwide. The specimen illustrated is from Jurassic rocks in North Yorkshire, UK.

Comments: *Williamsonia* bore cones resembling flowers at the stem ends. Both ovules and pollen were carried on the same plants. The leaves are often preserved as carbon films on bedding planes, as shown here.

CONTINENTAL DRIFT

The occurrence of abundant fossils of *Glossopteris* on now widely separated continents attracted the attention of Alfred Wegener (1880–1930) when he was putting together evidence for the drifting of the continents in his classic book *The Origin of the Continents* in 1924. He used many lines of evidence for the existence of the supercontinent called Gondwanaland and its split into the landmasses we know today, with the distribution of *Glossopteris* fossils being a key argument. He was not a geologist but a meteorologist, and the geological establishment scorned his elegant theory. They suggested that 'land bridges' must have existed, along which flora and fauna could migrate. Nowadays the ideas about continental drift are enhanced by plate tectonics theory. The Earth's crust and a small thickness of the mantle form 'plates' that can be shown to move and carry the land masses with them. *Glossopteris* fossils have their current distribution because Gondwanaland, where the plants flourished, has broken up and the fragments drifted apart on these plates.

GINKGO

Unlike the related Bennittitales, cycads such as *Ginkgo* have the male and female reproductive parts on different plants. The female tree has ovules and cones and the male bears sporangia. Typical leaves are triangular, or fan-shaped (see image on p.46), with deep

splits in them. The fossil record contains leaves almost identical to those on the modern species *Ginkgo biloba*.

Size: Today *ginkgos* may grow to 30m (100ft). The leaves shown are 25mm (1in) across.

Occurrence: Found worldwide in strata of Permian to Recent age. This specimen is from the Jurassic period of North Yorkshire, UK.

Comments: The maidenhair tree *Ginkgo biloba* lives wild in some regions of China today.

SALIX

This fossil leaf is from an ancient willow and belongs to the angiosperm group. These are modern flowering plants. The angiosperms began to develop in the Cretaceous period, and diversified during the Cenozoic era. *Salix* leaves vary between species, but typically have a central axis with main and subsidiary veins.

Size: The specimen illustrated is 30mm (1⅛in) long.

Occurrence: The genus is found worldwide in strata ranging from Eocene to Recent. The specimen is from the Eocene rocks of Colorado, USA.

Comments: *Salix* lives in cool temperate climates, with some species in cold climates. Pollen is very durable, and many plants are restricted to certain climatic conditions. Microscopic analysis of peat and other deposits reveals pollen grains, the identification of which allows the climate of the time to be worked out.

ACER

A genus from the angiosperm group, *Acer* is related to modern sycamores and maples. The leaves have a main point and less prominent side points. There is a central vein and many lesser veins. As a deciduous tree, *Acer* produces fresh leaves every year.

Size: The leaf shown is 50mm (2in) wide.

Occurrence: This genus is found worldwide in strata of Eocene to Recent age. The specimen shown (see image on opposite page) is from rocks of Miocene age in northern France.

Comments: The characteristic fruit consists of two seeds, each with a long 'wing' attached.

AMBER

Amber is the hardened resin that once seeped from trees. Preserved in sedimentary rocks, and frequently containing fossil insects, amber is known from strata as old as the Cretaceous period, and occurs in rocks of this age in New Jersey, Siberia, Canada and Burma. Around the Baltic, sediments formed during Eocene time contain amber, while Oligocene amber comes from Mexico. It can be difficult to tell the exact age of amber, though a study of the insects and other creatures fossilized within it helps to assess its age. Pines are the trees most likely to secrete the resin that becomes amber, with most resin produced during the warmer seasons. Amber is used commercially for jewellery.

ABOVE: This polished specimen (left), about 25mm (1in) across, contains a fossilized insect. The rough, unpolished piece of amber (right) is about 50mm (2in) wide.

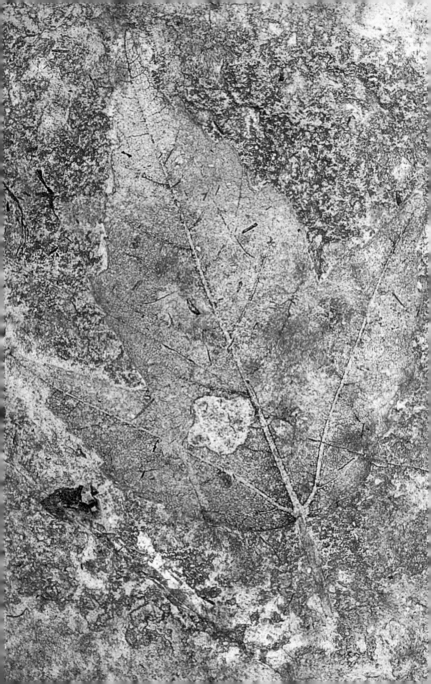

CORALS AND SPONGES

Corals are easily fossilized, and their calcareous structures are ready-made limestone. They are classified within the phylum Cnidaria and the class Anthozoa. Three groups of corals are commonly found in the fossil record – the Tabulata, Rugosa and Scleractinia. The first two of these groups are now extinct, but the scleractinian corals evolved during the Triassic period and are important reef-builders today.

A coral builds a tube or cone-shaped structure from calcium carbonate, in the top part (the calice) of which the soft-bodied coral polyp lives. Corals are closely related to sea anemones, and the coral animal is similar in form. Within the coral there are various structures that are valuable in distinguishing genera and species from each other, as are the general size and shape of the coral. Calcite plates called tabulae divide the coral horizontally. These can be flat or arched. Radiating from the central axis of the coral are vertical sheets called septa. These appear like the spokes in a wheel when seen from above. Septa are often in definite patterns in different species, and so are of diagnostic value. Many corals have around the inner margin of the corallite a web-like mass of calcite. This is made up of dissepiments, which strengthen the coral.

Tabulate corals are in many respects the simplest. They tend to have a small, calcareous corallite, which can be either branching, or joined in colonies by small, tube-like extensions. These corals rarely have septa, but typically have tabulae formed as horizontal or domed calcareous plates. First appearing in the Ordovician period, the tabulate corals became extinct during the Permian. They were at their most numerous during the Silurian and Carboniferous periods.

Rugose corals may be either solitary or linked in colonies. Their name comes from the series of ridges that often occur on the outside of the corallite wall. Internally, they are more complex than the tabulate corals, having both tabulae and septa. Around the margins of the corallite wall there are often dissepiments built in a web-like mass. These corals are first found as fossils in rocks of

OPPOSITE: This polished **Lonsdaleia** *specimen from South Wales, UK, shows the internal structure of septa and dissepiments.*

Ordovician age and, like the tabulates, they became extinct in the Permian period. In the Lower Carboniferous limestones, rugose corals are very numerous, and some species are used as zone fossils.

Scleractinian corals may be either solitary or colonial. They are often referred to as hexacorals, because the internal septa occur in groups of six. Like the rugose corals, scleratinians may have dissepiments. The solitary scleractinian corals have a cylindrical or cone-shaped corallite, but the colonial forms are very variable. These corals evolved during the Triassic period and flourished in the Jurassic, often being important reef-builders. They are still numerous today, especially in warm oceans.

CORAL ANATOMY

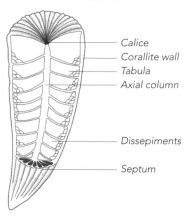

Calice
Corallite wall
Tabula
Axial column

Dissepiments

Septum

CORALS

THAMNOPORA

A tabulate coral that grew in large colonies standing up on a shallow seabed, probably growing among mounds of stromatoporoids (extinct Porifera). The individual corallites have a rounded cross-section, and often branch. The internal tabulae – the horizontal divisions within the corallite – are thin and often widely spaced, but the walls of the corallite are relatively thick. The internal tabulae and short, spinose septa can be seen in this cut and polished specimen.

Size: The corallites grew to 100mm (4in).
Occurrence: This genus is found in rocks of Devonian age, worldwide. The specimen is from Torquay, Devon, UK.
Comments: Usually the colonies were near reefs but not contributing to them. *Thamnopora* is often associated with other corals and brachiopods, which all contributed to limestone formation.

HALYSITES

The so-called 'chain coral' *Halysites* is a tabulate, colonial coral with many small corallites linked on two or three sides in a sinuous chain. The individual corallites are rounded or ovoid in cross-section and have flat or arching tabulae. Short, spinose septa may be present, but many individuals lack septa.

Size: The small corallites are about 2mm (1⁄12 in) in diameter. Whole colonies may reach 100mm (4in) in diameter.

Occurrence: This genus occurs in rocks of Ordovician and Silurian age, worldwide. The specimen illustrated is from Silurian limestones in Shropshire, UK.

Comments: *Halysites* is well known as a reef-building coral, and is found in limestones with a rich fauna of molluscs, trilobites, brachiopods and other corals.

FAVOSITES

A colonial tabulate coral with a massive, rounded shape, its surface is covered with small, tightly packed corallites. These are polygonal

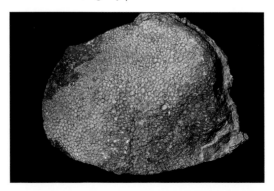

in cross-section, thin-walled and porous. Inside the corallites there may be short, spiny septa. Complex tabulae divide the corallite vertically. *Favosites* is sometimes called a 'honeycomb' coral.

Size: Whole colonies may reach 150mm (6in) in diameter.

Occurrence: *Favosites* occurs in shallow-water limestones of Ordovician to Devonian age, in North America, Europe, Asia and Australasia.

Comments: This common coral is best known from Silurian rocks. The specimen shown is of this age, from Shropshire, UK.

KODONOPHYLLUM

This is a solitary tabulate coral. The overall structure is that of an elongate cone, growing from a narrow base. The corallite walls are externally rough and there is a deep calice at the top. Internally, the incomplete tabulae often have an arched structure. The corallite walls are not strengthened with dissepiments and the septa are weak.

CORALS AND SPONGES

Size: The specimen illustrated is typical at 50mm (2in) in height.
Occurrence: A genus from Ordovician to Devonian strata in
North America, Asia and Europe. It is best known from
Silurian limestones.
Comments: This genus occurs typically in shallow-water limestones
with an assoc-iated fauna of brachiopods, molluscs and other corals.

LONSDALEIA

A colonial rugose coral, *Lonsdaleia* has its corallite walls thickened
by a mass of dissepiments. Other internal structures include septa,
which radiate from the thickened axial column. The horizontal tabulae are slightly concave, and there is a marked central calice. The
tightly packed colonies of this genus often form broad sheets that
can be followed for many miles along particular strata.

Size: The field of view is about 80mm (3⅛ in).
Occurrence: This coral is from Carboniferous strata in North America, North Africa, Australia and Europe.
Comments: The genus is thought to have lived in shallow,
reasonably warm, marine conditions, in which lime mud readily
accumulated. This mud later became limestone.

DIBUNOPHYLLUM

This solitary rugose coral is shown in a cut and polished specimen. The radiating septa and wall-thickening dissepiments are clearly seen. Both long and shorter septa are present, and there are also horizontal tabulae. The axis in the centre of the corallite is very complex and takes up about a third of the coral. It has a structure not unlike the dissepiments and is rather like a spider's web.

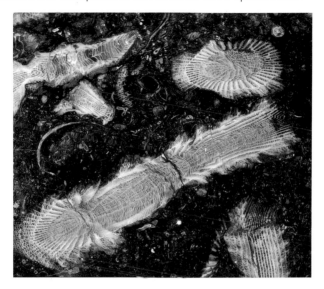

Size: A relatively large coral, the genus grew to a diameter of about 50mm (2in).
Occurrence: Found in Carboniferous rocks in North America, Asia and Europe. The specimen illustrated is from Durham, UK.
Comments: A widespread and common coral in continental-shelf limestones. It occurs regularly with other corals, molluscs and brachiopods.

ACERVULARIA

A colonial rugose coral with large individual corallites. The corallite margins are very thick where the dissepiments and septa become fused together. The corallites usually have four sides. A zone of flat-plated dissepiments has globular structures on either side. The

tabulae are slightly convex. *Acervularia* is a well-known coral in shallow-water limestones.

Size: The individual corallites can be 15mm (⅗in) in diameter.

Occurrence: A genus that is found in rocks of Silurian age in North America and Europe.

Comments: *Acervularia* typically occurs in limestones and shales with an associated fauna of trilobites, brachiopods, molluscs and other corals.

CYATHOPHYLLUM

This solitary rugose coral has considerable variation in structure. The outside surface of the corallite walls is uneven, with many stout ridges, a typical feature of rugose corals (see image on opposite page). The calice at the top of the corallite is shallow. Internally, the septa virtually reach the axial column and the corallite walls are strengthened with numerous rounded dissepiments. The tabulae vary from concave to flat.

Size: The shorter specimen shown is 50mm (2in) long.

Occurrence: This genus is found in rocks of Devonian age in North America, Asia, Europe and Australia.

Comments: The illustration shows a typical cone-shaped structure and a slender form. Limestones often contain fossil coral in their position of growth. Lime mud accumulating on the seabed around living coral can turn to limestone relatively quickly.

KETOPHYLLUM

Typical uneven ridges are evident on the outer surface of this corallite. Its overall shape is like a narrow cone, and some individuals have small, root-like structures which anchored them to the sea floor. The specimen illustrated has been cut to show its internal structure. A thick layer of dissepiments on the margin of the corallite wall can be seen. The horizontal tabulae bend upwards at their margins, where the dissepiments are dominant. Incomplete septa divide the corallite vertically. This specimen contains much pale, crystalline calcite.

Size: The example shown is 80mm (3⅛in) tall.
Occurrence: Found in strata of Silurian age in China and Europe. The specimen is from Shropshire, UK.
Comments: This solitary rugose coral is one of the genera used to work out the number of days in the Silurian year (see box on p.64).

SIPHONODENDRON

A colonial rugose coral in which the individual corallites are very near each other, *Siphonodendron* has all the characteristic features of rugose corals. In this sectioned example the central axis can be clearly seen. Radiating from this are numerous septa which reach to the corallite wall. About a quarter of the corallite contains dissepiments growing inwards from the wall.

Size: The individuals in this typical example are 6mm (¼in) in diameter.

Occurrence: *Siphonodendron* is found in strata of Carboniferous age in Europe.

Comments: This genus occurs in limestones and other shallow-water continental shelf deposits.

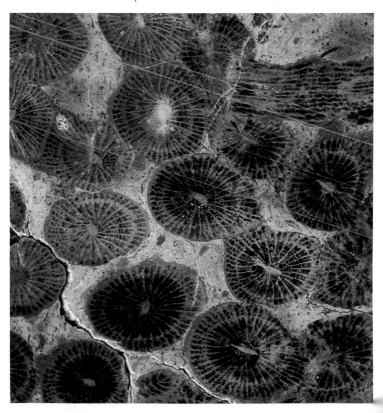

SYRINGOPORA

This colonial tabulate coral has a far less complex structure than colonial rugose corals. It grew in extensive colonies in shallow seas, and is typically found in limestone. The individual corallites have thick walls and are joined by thinner calcareous tubes called tubuli. Internally there may be small, pointed septa radiating from the centre, and concave tabulae.

Size: The illustrated specimen is about 100mm (4in) across.

Occurrence: *Syringopora* is well known from rocks of Carboniferous age, but is also found in the Silurian and Devonian systems, worldwide.

Comments: *Syringopora* often occurs fossilized with encrusting stromatoporoids, but it also lived away from these organisms.

THYSANOPHYLLUM

Thysanophyllum is a colonial rugose coral. The corallites, which vary in size, are stuck together closely so that they virtually share corallite walls. These are strengthened by dissepiments, and the radiating septa run from the central axis to the corallite walls. The calice is slightly depressed. The shape of each corallite is either hexagonal or octagonal, giving the whole colony an angular internal appearance.

Size: The field of view in the illustration is 85mm (3⅜in).

Occurrence: This genus is from strata of Carboniferous age in Europe.

Comments: Its main features can be seen well in this slightly weathered specimen.

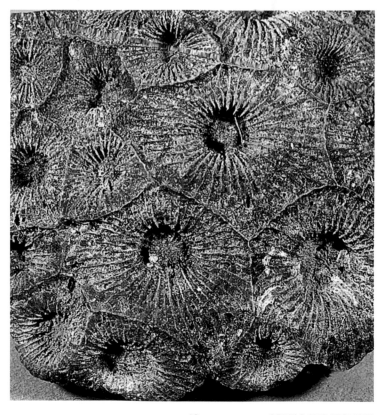

CORALS AS FOSSIL CLOCKS

Because corals secrete a calcite structure they are fossilized in great detail, often virtually as they grew. Their individual growth patterns can be readily worked out. Both rugose and scleractinian corals show minute growth ridges, in some cases as many as 200 per centimetre. These are called 'growth increments'. Modern corals develop around 360 of these growth increments each year. The structures are grouped in bands that represent monthly accretions of coral, and wider bands that are annual markers. A study of the Silurian coral *Ketophyllum* shows that it has growth increments in annual groups of 400. *Lithostrotion* from the Carboniferous period has 398. This all suggests that there were more days in the year in the distant past and that each day was shorter. Confirmation comes from astronomy, which shows that the Earth's movement round the Sun has changed by almost exactly the amount the fossil corals show.

CANINIA

This solitary rugose coral shows typical external ridges on the corallite wall. Usually the corallite is tube-shaped, but cone-shaped forms are also found. The radiating septa are shown well on this weathered specimen, both spreading from the central axis and running vertically down the corallite. The tabulae are flat, but concave towards the corallite wall, which is thickened with dissepiments. This specimen has been partly altered to pinkish quartz during fossilization.

Size: A medium to large coral, it may grow to 100mm (4in) or more in height.
Occurrence: This genus is found in strata of Carboniferous age in North America, Europe, North Africa, Australia and Asia.
Comments: It commonly occurs in shallow- water limestones, associated with a reef-building fauna.

THECOSMILIA

A scleractinian coral that can have branching corallites. These may grow in small colonies or individually. Two individuals are illustrated, one branching, the other simple. *Thecosmilia* has septa radiating from the centre. These septa are in groups of six – a typical feature of scleractian corals. (For this reason they are often called hexacorals.) The septa can be seen as thin, sharp ridges running vertically down each specimen. The corallite walls are strengthened with dissepiments.

Size: The specimens shown are typical at 50mm (2in) across.
Occurrence: The genus ranges from Triassic to Cretaceous, and is found worldwide. The specimen shown is from Gloucestershire, UK.
Comments: *Thecosmilia* is common in limestone reef deposits of Jurassic age, which were formed in warm, shallow seas.

ISASTRAEA

This specimen is a colony of numerous small scleractinian corallites. The individuals can be seen packed together with their six-sided corallite walls fused. The overall structure is a rough-sided, unbranched cylinder that grew on the seabed, from its narrow base. The numerous septa radiate in groups of six from the centre of the corallites. In some species the septa reach out through the corallite walls to join with neighbouring individuals. Dissepiments strengthen each corallite wall.

Size: The illustrated specimen is typical at 100mm (4in) in height.

Occurrence: This genus is found in strata of Jurassic and Cretaceous age in North America, Africa and Europe.

Comments: It is associated with other corals in reef structures that formed in warm, shallow seas. These reefs were a favourable habitat for many other organisms found fossilized with the corals. These include molluscs, brachiopods, echinoderms and sponges.

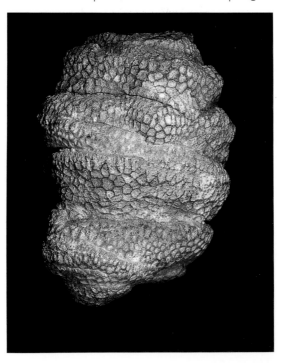

THAMNASTREA

A colonial coral genus, *Thamnastrea* is unusual because corallite walls are lacking and individual corallites simply fuse with each other. This feature is easily seen in the sectioned specimen illustrated. The thin axial structure can also be seen. The overall form is that of a slender, twig-like, branched corallite.

Size: Individual corals are typically up to 100mm (4in) long.

Occurrence: In rocks of Triassic and Jurassic age, *Thamnastrea* is often found with other genera such as *Isastrea*. It occurs in North America, South America, Europe and Asia.

Comments: The reefs formed by this and other scleractinian corals grew to 2m (6½ft) across.

CORALS AND SPONGES

SPONGES

These organisms are classified in the phylum Porifera, and even though they have a relatively soft structure, they are not uncommon as fossils. Sponges are among the simplest multi-celled organisms, having simple, sack-like bodies that are supported by small, internal spines called spicules. These can be made of silica, and when this is the case they are readily fossilized. (Some genera have spicules made of calcite.) Silica from sponge spicules is a major constituent of rocks such as chert, a material that is found as nodules in many limestones. Externally the sponge is porous, and water containing food and oxygen is sucked in through the pores. The geological record of sponges begins in the Cambrian period, and they are common in marine conditions today.

SPONGE STRUCTURE

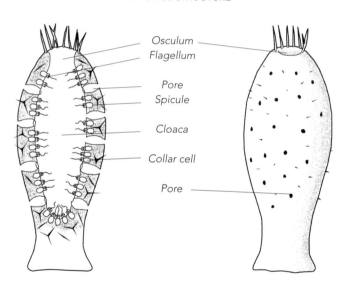

Osculum
Flagellum

Pore
Spicule

Cloaca

Collar cell

Pore

RAPHIDONEMA

This genus has an open structure widening from a narrow base, and is almost vase-shaped. The walls are thick and very porous, the pores being clearly seen in the illustration. It is a calcareous sponge. On the outer surface there are numerous ridges and lumps, giving a very rough texture.

Size: *Raphidonema* grew to around 50mm (2in) in height.

Occurrence: This sponge is found in rocks of Triassic, Jurassic and Cretaceous age in Europe. The specimen shown is from Kent, UK.

Comments: This genus lived in shallow marine conditions, and was anchored to the seabed by its narrow base.

SIPHONIA

Siphonia has an overall shape very similar to that of a partly opened tulip flower. The upper part is rounded, narrowing to the top, and it is supported on the seabed by a slender stem, with numerous 'roots' at its base. As in the specimen illustrated, this stem is often broken in fossils. *Siphonia* is a sponge with siliceous spicules supporting its structure. The thick wall is porous, and internally there is a complex system of canals for the movement of seawater through the organism. Some canals are radial, others parallel to the sponge walls.

Size: Typically *Siphonia* was 80mm (3⅛in) tall.

Occurrence: This sponge is found in rocks of Cretaceous and

CORALS AND SPONGES

Cenozoic age in Europe and Australia.
Comments: Sponges such as *Siphonia* are able to bore into limestone and shell material.

SELISCOTHON

This genus is a siliceous sponge with spicules made of silica. The body of the sponge is rather flat and not unlike a mushroom. A root-like structure anchored it to the seabed. As can be seen in the illustration, the surface is covered with pores. The name *Laosciadia* has also been used for this genus.

Size: The specimen shown is typical at about 50mm (2in) in diameter.
Occurrence: A genus that occurs in Cretaceous rocks in Europe.
Comments: The nodules of flint that form as regular bands within the chalk of Cretaceous age are made of silica. Much of this is probably derived from sponge spicules, and sponges such as Seliscothon are often found fossilized within flint nodules.

VENTRICULITES

Ventriculites is shaped like an inverted cone. The specimen illustrated has been flattened during fossilization. The internal structure supporting the sponge is made from siliceous spicules, which are fused to give a solid 'skeleton'.

Size: Typically *Ventriculites* grew to about 50mm (2in) in height.

Occurrence: A genus found in Cretaceous rocks in Europe.

Comments: This sponge is attached to the seabed by thin 'roots'. As seen in the illustration, the outer surface can be covered with rows of indentations, giving a rough texture.

ECHINODERMS

Creatures within this phylum are found fossilized in strata dating back to the Cambrian period. Today they are common in many different marine environments. Essentially echinoderms have an exoskeleton, which can be spinose, and their symmetry is often pentameral (five-fold). There are four classes in the phylum commonly found as fossils.

The **echinoids** (sea urchins) have an exoskeleton, the test, which varies in shape between the genera. It can be rounded, flattened or even heart-shaped, and this shape is usually related to the way of life of the creature. The test is made of numerous calcite plates interlocking along zigzag sutures. The surface is covered with spines. In some genera these are small and almost fur-like, in others they are fewer and club-shaped. The ambulacra (five narrow bands of plates) have pores through which small tube feet pass. These

ECHINOID STRUCTURE (LATERAL CROSS-SECTION)

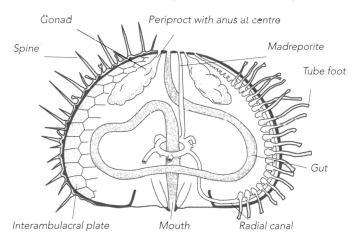

OPPOSITE: Crinoidal limestone. The stems of crinoids break easily into individual ossicles. Much limestone of Carboniferous age is composed of crinoid fragments. This specimen, from Durham, UK, contains crinoid stem fragments, brachiopods and bryozoans.

are linked to the internal water vascular system, and are used for movement and respiration. On the end of each tube foot is a small rounded sucker. In some genera the ambulacra run right round the test, while in others they can be atrophied or even petal-shaped. On the underside (the oral surface) of the test, often in the centre, is a group of plates called the peristome, which surrounds the mouth. The anus is usually on the opposite side of the test, on the upper (aboral) surface. It is surrounded by the periproct, a series of relatively large plates.

Two distinct types of echinoids are recognized. The regular echinoids have a rounded test with the anus and mouth centrally placed, and encircling ambulacra. Their symmetry is five-fold. The irregular echinoids (which probably evolved from the regular ones) have bilateral symmetry, with the mouth and anus often no longer central, and the ambulacra may be atrophied.

Crinoids are also called 'sea lilies' because of their plant-like habit. They are delicate organisms, with a stem made of calcite plates called ossicles. At the base of this, 'roots' anchor the animal

CRINOID STRUCTURE

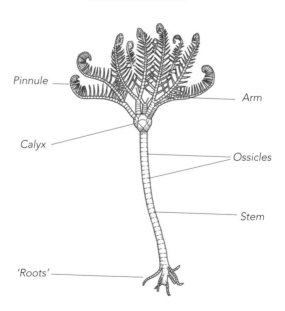

Pinnule

Arm

Calyx

Ossicles

Stem

'Roots'

to the seabed. A cup-like calyx is at the top of the stem and in this the animal lived. Branching, ciliated arms rise above the calyx, directing water currents towards the mouth. The remains of crinoids are common in many rocks, especially limestones, where their broken stems often contribute to the sediment.

The starfish and brittle stars are classified as **asteroids** and **ophiuroids**. They are not as common in the fossil record as the other echinoderms, possibly because they are so delicate. Nevertheless, there are a number of notable examples of 'starfish beds' crowded with the remains of asteroids. Many fossil starfish are very similar to modern forms, especially the brittle stars, which seem to have remained virtually the same for hundreds of millions of years.

ABOVE: Crinoidal limestone. The stems of crinoids break easily into individual ossicles. Much limestone of Carboniferous age is composed of crinoid fragments. This specimen, from Durham, UK, contains crinoid stem fragments, brachiopods and bryozoans.

ECHINODERMS

CRINOIDS, STARFISH AND ECHINOIDS

SCYPHOCRINITES

Scyphocrinites has a relatively short stem with a rounded structure at its base. This is made of numerous plates similar to the ossicles from which the stem is built. The purpose of this basal structure is not known for certain. However, there is some evidence that it may have been a float, and so this genus could have been carried by ocean currents. The calyx is made of larger plates at its base and smaller ones towards the upper part from where the arms develop.

Size: A large crinoid, *Scyphocrinites* grew to over a metre (39in) in height.

Occurrence: A crinoid that has been found in Silurian and Devonian strata in North America, Europe, Asia and Africa.

Comments: This genus has a very wide geographical range, and may have been moved by ocean currents. In some areas it is very common, and ossicles have accumulated in vast numbers to form

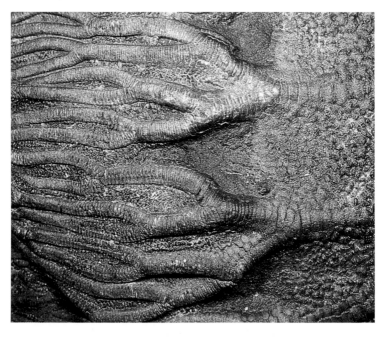

scyphocrinite limestone in some parts of Oklahoma and Missouri, USA. The specimen shown is from Devonian strata in Alnif, North Africa. Scyphocrinite limestones are also well known in the Carnic Alps in Austria.

MACROCRINUS

Macrocrinus has a slender stem composed of rounded ossicles. Set above this is the calyx, which is cup-shaped and made of large plates, with a stout, rounded structure at the base. Above the calyx are 12 to 16 arms. These (as seen here) have numerous pinnules, making the arms look like feathers.

Size: Whole specimens reached around 50mm (2in) in height.

Occurrence: A crinoid that occurs in the Carboniferous of North America. This specimen is from Indiana, USA.

Comments: This crinoid is commonly found in shallow-water limestones.

WOODOCRINUS

Only the calyx and arms of this crinoid are shown (see image on p.78). The calyx is small. The point where the stem joined it can be seen at the base. The stem is rounded and tapering, and is without 'roots' to anchor it into the seabed. The arms above the calyx each branch from triangular plates into two smaller branches.

ECHINODERMS

Size: A complete specimen of *Woodocrinus* is around 100mm (4in) in height.

Occurrence: This genus is found in Carboniferous strata in Europe.

Comments: A number of species of *Woodocrinus* have been described. They differ in the detailed structure of their arms and calyx.

PENTACRINITES

This genus is perhaps best known for its star-shaped ossicles. As with most crinoids, the stem is very brittle, the ossicles readily breaking apart to be fossilized individually. The stem is very long and some forms are anchored to the seabed, while others are free-swimming. The calyx is small, but it has numerous long, branching arms, which are covered in pinnules. Fossils are sometimes found in great numbers, forming masses on certain strata.

Size: *Pentacrinites* can be over a metre (39in) long.

Occurrence: First found fossilized in Triassic strata it and still survives today. Fossil specimens occur in North America and Europe.

Comments: The modern species of this genus become free-swimming in the adult stage, having been anchored when young.

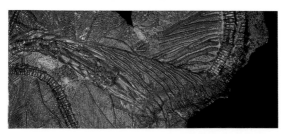

CLEMATOCRINUS

In this rather fragmented specimen, which is typical of the preservation of many crinoids, part of the calyx and the arms are preserved. The ossicles of the stem have broken up. *Clematocrinus* has thin, branching arms that are covered in pinnules. 'Roots' anchored the slender stem to the seabed.

Size: The illustrated specimen is 25mm (1in) long.

Occurrence: This crinoid genus occurs in strata of Silurian age in North America, Europe and Australia.

Comments: It is found in limestones, many of which were formed in shallow marine conditions. The associated fauna is characteristic of reefs, and includes corals, bryozoans and brachiopods.

ENCRINUS

This well-known crinoid has almost perfect pentameral (five-fold) symmetry. The calyx is fairly flat and cup-shaped. It is made of a number of large, five-sided basal plates with two rows of smaller plates above. The long, slender stem, composed of circular ossicles and joined to a depression below the calyx, is not often preserved unbroken. Rising above the calyx are ten arms. These are made of single plates initially, but these double in number, and eventually the slender tops of the arms are again made of single plates.

Size: The whole crinoid is about 75mm (3in) in height.

Occurrence: This genus is found in marine Triassic strata in Europe. It is especially well known from the Muschelkalk of Germany. Here

ECHINODERMS

Orepanaster is found in such beds. Near Girvan in southern Scotland, UK, is the 'Girvan starfish bed'. This is an Ordovician calcareous sandstone containing, in addition to brittle stars, many well-preserved fossils such as trilobites, molluscs, echinoids, corals and brachiopods. A detailed study of the sedimentary rock in which the fossils are contained, and of sediment within some of the fossils, shows that the deposit was carried by rapid, shallow-sea currents.

LAPWORTHURA

Lapworthura has the typical ophiuroid structure, comprising a central disc and radiating arms. The disc contains five pointed structures from which the sinuous arms branch out. The arms, which assisted movement, are fragile, often being broken in fossils. In this

genus they have a serrated edge with small, feathery spines.

Size: This grew to a maximum of around 100mm (4in) in diameter.

Occurrence: It is found in rocks of Ordovician and Silurian age in Europe and Australia.

Comments: Modern ophiuroids have a very similar structure to that of *Lapworthura* occurring in Palaeozoic rocks. They have been a very successful group since then, and have somehow avoided the major mass extinctions that affected so many groups at certain times.

PALAEOCOMA

This ophiuroid has been fossilized in a mass. The central structure contains ten triangular plates. From each pair of these radiate the arms, which are long and slender, tapering gradually to a point and bearing poorly developed spines. In some individuals, the arms can be seen reaching to the centre of the organism.

Size: A whole individual may reach 100mm (4in) in diameter.

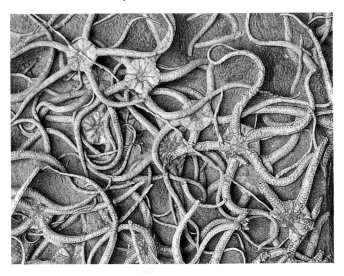

Occurrence: *Palaeocoma* occurs in rocks of Jurassic and Cretaceous age, worldwide. This specimen is from lower Jurassic strata in Dorset, UK.

Comments: This genus has many similarities to today's brittle stars, which can be found in shallow marine environments and in rock pools left at low tide.

METOPASTER

This unusual asteroid (starfish) has no definite arms. There is a typical five-fold symmetry that is shown by the organization of the large plates that make up the border. These plates are often found as isolated fossils, looking rather like teeth. Those covering the body vary in structure. Underneath there is a series of organized plates with ambulacral and interambulacral areas. Above, however, a mass of very small, irregular plates occurs, seen in the illustration below.

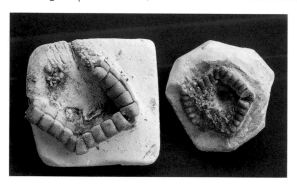

Size: *Metopaster* grew to 50mm (2in) in diameter.
Occurrence: This genus occurs in Cretaceous to Miocene strata in North America, New Zealand and Europe.
Comments: Starfish such as *Metopaster* show a very slow evolution through the fossil record.

CLYPEUS

This irregular echinoid has a flattened test divided by narrow, petaloid ambulacra radiating from the centre of the test that have thin,

slit-shaped pores along their margins. On the aboral surface there is a deep groove running from the perimeter of the test almost to the centre. This contains the anus. The oral surface has a sub-central mouth. The whole surface of the test is covered with small pores.

Size: *Clypeus* grew to a diameter of around 100mm (4in)

Occurrence: This is a common genus in Jurassic strata in Europe, Africa and Australia.

Comments: *Clypeus* has a similar structure to that of certain modern echinoids and probably lived on the seabed in relatively calm conditions.

CIDARIS

Cidaris is a regular echinoid. The test has a rounded outline, and the mouth and anus are centrally placed. The ambulacral plates form narrow rows. There are massive bosses on the test, marking the positions where the large, club-shaped spines were anchored. These are often found as separate fossils. The test also has various other forms of ornamentation, mainly small tubercles and pores.

Size: A genus that grew to around 30mm (1⅛in).

Occurrence: *Cidaris* occurs in strata from Jurassic to Recent age, worldwide.

Comments: In modern species of this genus, the spines are used for moving along the seabed.

ECHINODERMS

PYGASTER

An irregular echinoid with a very flattened test covered in small tubercles. In life the test was coated with short spines. The echinoid has a pentagonal outline and the thin ambulacral areas are almost straight. The anus is non-central, with the periproct (the group of plates normally surrounding the anus) being shaped like a keyhole.

Size: The specimen shown is typical at 60mm (2⅖in) in diameter.
Occurrence: *Pygaster* is found in strata of Jurassic and Cretaceous age in Europe.
Comments: As with many of the irregular echinoids, *Pygaster* burrowed into seabed sediment. Fossil evidence suggests it lived in mud and oolitic sediment eroded from shallow reefs.

MICRASTER

This well-known genus has been the subject of many detailed studies, especially looking at its evolution into different species during the Cretaceous period. With time, the genus evolved with a higher, wider test and the ambulacra lengthened. The anterior groove became deeper and the mouth gradually evolved to a

more forward position. *Micraster* has a characteristic heart-shaped test, covered in small bosses, in which the oral and aboral surfaces differ considerably. The ambulacra are petaloid and stunted, occurring only on the aboral surface. The anus is placed high at the posterior end of the test, and on the oral surface the mouth has a pronounced labrum (lip) above it. At the posterior end of the oral surface, leading away behind the labrum, there is a wide flattened area, the plastron, covered with closely packed tubercles.

Size: Typically the genus grew to 50mm (2in) in diameter.

Occurrence: *Micraster* is found in strata of Cretaceous and Palaeocene age in Europe, North Africa, Madagascar and Cuba.

Comments: It was a burrowing echinoid, very similar to the living *Echinocardium*, which burrows into soft sediment and is often found washed up on the shore. According to comparative studies, different species in the evolutionary sequence of *Micraster* probably burrowed to different depths.

ECHINOCORYS

This is an irregular echinoid with a dome-shaped test. The base of the test is flat and, from above, its outline is oval. It thus has bilateral symmetry. The ambulacra are nearly straight and have two parallel bands of pores. Interambulacral areas are broad, with a covering of small tubercles. The mouth has a crescent-shaped opening and is at the anterior end of the oral surface, while the anus is near the posterior end, opposite the mouth. Fewer pores are present on the oral surface.

Size: *Echinocorys* grew to around 80mm (3⅛in) in diameter.

Occurrence: Found in rocks of Cretaceous and Palaeocene age in North America, Europe, Russia and Madagascar.

ECHINODERMS

Comments: This genus lived in shallow burrows in the soft, chalky mud of the seabed.

HEMIPNEUSTES

An irregular echinoid with a high, dome-shaped test, *Hemipneustes* has bilateral symmetry. The convex upper surface is smooth, with narrow, curving ambulacral areas, each containing two rows of slit-like pores. The anterior ambulacrum follows a groove as it passes below the edge of the test. The peristome (the series of plates normally surrounding the mouth) is crescent-shaped and positioned anteriorly on the oral surface. The periproct and anus are both on this surface.
Size: One of the larger Cretaceous echinoids, the genus grew to over 100mm (4in) in diameter.

Occurrence: *Hemipneustes* is fossilized in strata of Cretaceous age in Europe.
Comments: Modern related genera live today in the Indian Ocean. They have been recorded at depths reaching 900m (3,000ft).

HOLECTYPUS

This irregular echinoid has a rounded outline from above, and is hemispherical when viewed from the side. The domed test is flattened to slightly concave on the oral surface, and the non-petaloid ambulacra are entire, reaching right around the test. Both the mouth and anus are on the oral surface. The anus is marginal in an oval periproct, but the exact position varies with different species. The mouth is central. The test has small tubercles, which are coarser on the oral surface.

Size: *Holectypus* grew to about 30mm (1⅛in) in diameter.
Occurrence: A genus from Jurassic and Cretaceous rocks in North America and Europe.
Comments: This genus shows features that may be in an evolutionary stage between regular and irregular echinoids.

DENDRASTER

The test is oval in outline and very flat. The stunted, petaloid ambulacra have parallel rows of slit-shaped pores. Radiating from the posteriorly positioned apical system, the ambulacra are shorter towards the posterior side of the test. A shallow groove leads from the apical system towards the anus on the oral surface.

Size: This genus reaches about 80mm (3⅛in) in diameter.
Occurrence: *Dendraster* is found in Cretaceous to Recent strata in North America. It is especially common in the Kettelman Hills area of California, USA, where fossil tests make up much of the rock.

89

Comments: This genus is often referred to as a 'sand dollar'. It lives with the anterior part of the test steeply buried in seabed sediment, and the posterior part protruding above the sediment into the seawater.

LOVENIA

This irregular echinoid has a heart-shaped test in some species, while in others it is more oval in outline. Seen from the side, the test has a vertical posterior margin, and the anus is situated high up on this part of the test. The mouth is slightly crescent-shaped and positioned anteriorly on the oral surface. The ambulacra are unusual: four of them are short and stubby, terminating on the aboral surface. The anterior ambulacrum is non-petaloid and less pronounced than the others, and runs in a shallow groove to the test margin. There are large depressed tubercles on the interambulacral areas.

Size: This genus grows to 50mm (2in) in diameter.
Occurrence: *Lovenia* is well known in strata of Eocene to Recent age in Australia.
Comments: Today it lives in a wide range of habitats, from shallow to deep sea, thinly covered by seabed sediment.

CLYPEASTER

An irregular echinoid with an oval or sub-pentagonal outline, *Clypeaster* is domed when viewed from the side. There are internal supporting structures. On the underside of the test is a deep central hollow where the peristome and mouth are situated. Five deep, slender furrows lead towards the mouth. Cilia in these

furrows create water currents carrying food. The anus is also on the oral surface at the posterior margin. Unusual ambulacra are a characteristic feature of *Clypeaster*. These are short and pear-shaped, radiating from the centre of the aboral surface. Their margins have slit-shaped pores.

Size: This is one of the largest echinoid genera, growing to 150mm (6in) in diameter.

Occurrence: *Clypeaster* occurs in rocks of Eocene to Recent age, worldwide.

Comments: Modern species live in shallow tropical seas, burrowing partially into sediment.

AMPHIOPE

This genus is an irregular echinoid with a very flattened test. The outline of the test is unusual: it is ovoid, but has two distinct notches in the posterior margin. The ambulacra are very short and petaloid. Large pores form a circle in the centre of the aboral surface from where the ambulacra radiate. On the oral surface the mouth is central, and branching grooves lead from the mouth towards the margin of the test. Also on the oral surface, the anus is on the posterior edge, midway between the two notches.

Size: The larger of the two specimens shown is 30mm (1⅛in) in diameter.

Occurrence: *Amphiope* is fossilized in rocks of Oligocene to Miocene age in Europe and India.

Comments: As with other echinoids that have very flat tests, this genus lived on the seabed.

ENCOPE

This irregular genus is recognized by its rounded test with large holes in it, five of these being at the ends of the petaloid ambulacra (see image on the opposite page). There are slit-like pores along the ambulacral margins. The mouth is central on the oral surface, with a series of furrows radiating from it. These furrows carry food to the mouth. The anus is also on the oral surface.

Size: A genus that grows to about 100mm (4in) in diameter.

Occurrence: *Encope* is found in rocks of Miocene to Recent age in North and South America and the West Indies. The illustrated specimen is from California, USA.

Comments: Living species of *Encope* have a mass of small spines covering the test, giving an almost fur-like appearance.

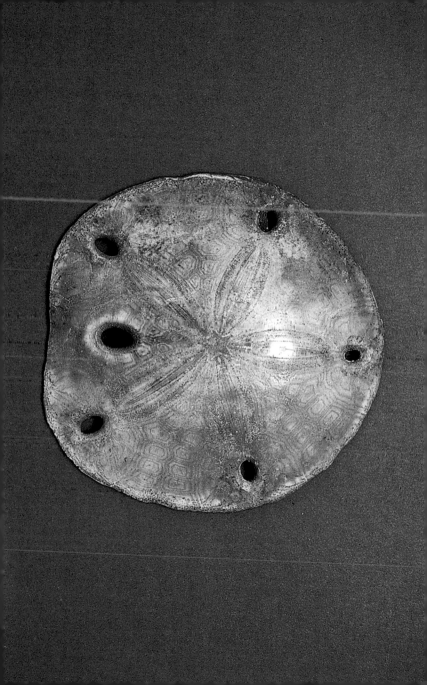

BRACHIOPODS

Brachiopods are a phylum of shelled organisms with a very long geological history. The first primitive brachiopods, such as *Lingulella*, are found in rocks of Cambrian age. Members of the phylum still live today in many marine environments, but there are far fewer of them now than at certain times in the past. Fossil brachiopods are found in many different sedimentary rocks, suggesting that the different genera were adapted to a variety of marine environments.

The shell of a brachiopod is composed of two valves. These are usually different from each other in size and structure. The pedicle valve, the larger one, has a small hole in it at its narrow end (the posterior end), through which a fleshy stalk called the pedicle protrudes. This anchors the brachiopod to the seabed, algae or another object. Some primitive brachiopods, such as *Lingula*, were burrowers, and the pedicle was then used to attach the shell to the bottom of the burrow. The smaller valve is the brachial valve. This has inside it a feeding apparatus called the lophophore, which is supported on a calcareous brachidium. The lophophore is covered with small, hair-like cilia on which food is trapped as seawater passes into the open anterior end of the shell. In the class called the Articulata (articulate brachiopods), the valves, made of fibrous calcite, can be opened by a set of diductor muscles and closed with adductor muscles. The less advanced class, the Inarticulata (inarticulate brachiopods), with a chitino-phosphatic shell, are not able to open and close their valves.

Bivalve molluscs (clams, oysters, tellins and their relatives) and brachiopods belong to two very distinct phyla. They are biologically different, though there are similarities in their shell structure, and there may be confusion in identifying fossil material. Both have two valves making up the shell. These may have growth lines, ribs and spines on the outer surface. Internally, most bivalves have two distinct muscle scars near the shell margin, which may be joined by a pallial line. Brachiopods have muscle scars in pairs nearer the beak and may also have a loop or spiral structure inside the shell.

OPPOSITE: A specimen of Silurian limestone from Shropshire, UK, containing the brachiopod **Leptaena** *(top) and many other small fossils, including other brachiopods and crinoid ossicles.*

The symmetry of the two phyla is distinct. In the bivalve molluscs the plane of symmetry lies between the two valves in most genera, and the valves are a mirror image of each other. In the brachiopods the valves are dissimilar, and the plane of symmetry cuts midway through each valve. One valve, the pedicle valve, is usually larger and has a hole in it for the pedicle; the brachial valve is generally smaller.

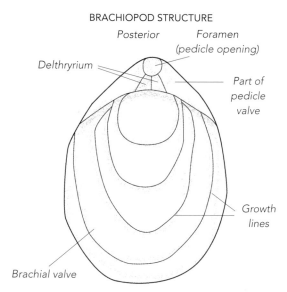

BRACHIOPOD STRUCTURE

LINGULA

This inarticulate brachiopod is recognized by its thin, oval shell, which is covered with concentric growth lines. Each valve is convex, and there is a relatively pronounced beak. The growth lines show the size of the shell when it was much smaller. Internally, the valves may have muscle scars. The two valves are much the same size and exhibit bilateral symmetry. The shell was chitino-phosphatic rather than having the calcareous structure of many brachiopods. In the illustration, pale brown original shell still adheres to some of the specimens.

Size: *Lingula* grows to around 40 mm (1⅜in) in length.
Occurrence: In strata ranging in age from Ordovician to Recent,

worldwide. The specimen is from strata of Carboniferous age in Northumbria, UK.

Comments: Today *Lingula* burrows up to 300mm (12in) deep into soft sediment. The shell is attached to its burrow by a long, fleshy pedicle. The slightly open anterior end of the shell is near the top of the burrow, allowing it to feed. If disturbed, the shell can be withdrawn by the pedicle contracting. It lives in marine and brackish water, and is a good indicator of environmental conditions.

LINGULELLA

Lingulella is very similar in many respects to *Lingula*, but its geological range is far shorter. The oval shell has faint growth lines and the valves are convex. Internally, there are delicate, radiating lines on the valves. The pedicle protrudes through a slight groove in the pedicle valve.

Size: This genus grew to around 30mm (1⅛in) in length.

Occurrence: In rocks of Cambrian and Ordovician age, worldwide. The specimen shown is from North Wales, UK.

BRACHIOPODS

Comments: Some species of this inarticulate genus may have been burrowers like *Lingula*, but others probably lived on the seabed.

SPIRIFER

This articulate brachiopod is characterized by a very straight hinge line. The valves are unequal in size, the pedicle valve being larger than the brachial valve. In the illustration, the pedicle valve is mostly hidden behind the brachial valve, except where it curves forwards to the hinge line. A fold (often called a sulcus) runs midway down the shell, and strong ribs radiate from the beak. Growth lines are faint, but can have small spines on them.

Size: This genus grew to around 40mm (1⅜in) in width.

Occurrence: *Spirifer* is found in Carboniferous age strata, worldwide.
Comments: Internally, the structure of *Spirifer* differs from that of many brachiopods. The brachidia, which support the feeding apparatus, the lophophore, are formed in a complex spiral. This can often be found in fossils when the valves are opened.

ORTHIS

This articulate brachiopod has a rounded outline to the valves. The convex pedicle valve is larger than the less convex brachial valve. Ribs radiating from the beak fan out towards the shell margins. The hinge line is straight, but is not the greatest shell width. There are pronounced muscle scars on the inside of the valves of some species.
Size: A small brachiopod that grew to around 20mm (⅘in) in width.
Occurrence: Found in strata of Ordovician age, worldwide.

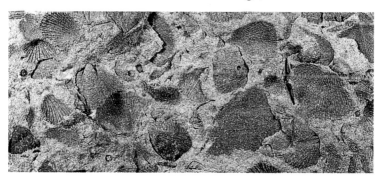

Comments: The illustration shows a mass of small *Orthis* shells preserved in micaceous sandstone from Shropshire, UK. This group of brachiopods possibly evolved into *Spirifer* and related genera.

ATRYPA

An articulate brachiopod with a rounded shell outline, *Atrypa* has a flattened pedicle valve and convex brachial valve (see image on p.100). The short hinge line is straight, and there is a slight flexure in the anterior part of the shell. The narrow, pointed beak curves over the anterior of the brachial valve. On the outside surface the shell is ornamented with radiating ribs and concentric growth lines. Internally, there is a complex brachidium coiled in a spiral.
Size: This genus grew to about 25mm (1in) in width.

Occurrence: *Atrypa* is found in strata of Silurian and Devonian age, worldwide.

Comments: The pedicle was used by juveniles to attach the shell to the seabed, but in adults its use was lost and the shell rested on the seabed on the brachial valve.

PRODUCTUS

This well-known articulate brachiopod has a semicircular shell outline and a straight hinge line. The pedicle valve is markedly convex, with a rounded beak, and the brachial valve flat or slightly concave.

The surface ornamentation consists of radiating ribs and wavy growth lines. There may also be small nodes and spines.

Size: A genus that grew to around 40mm (1⅜in) in width. Related genera such as *Gigantoproductus* grew to over 150mm (6in).

Occurrence: Found in strata of Ordovician to Permian age, worldwide.

Comments: The spines can be of considerable length (much longer than the shell in some species) and were used to anchor the brachiopod to soft sediment on the seabed.

LEPTAENA

Leptaena is an articulate brachiopod characterized by a convex pedicle valve and concave brachial valve. The shell outline is roughly rectangular, and the hinge line is straight, with extensions at both ends. The shell ornamentation consists of concentric ridges, which are wavy in some examples. Radiating from the beak are numerous fine striations. The posterior part of the shell bends with a very steep curve.

Size: This genus grew to about 50mm (2in) in width.

Occurrence: Found in strata of Ordovician, Silurian and Devonian age, worldwide.

Comments: *Leptaena* is common in limestones that formed on shallow continental shelves.

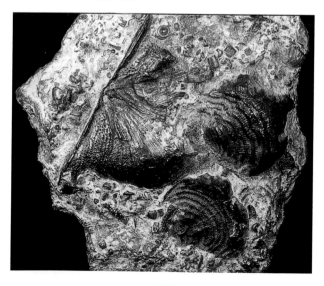

ORBICULOIDEA

This genus belongs to the inarticulate group of brachiopods. The valves have a circular outline with a cone-shaped brachial valve and flat pedicle valve. Two brachial valves are seen in the illustration. A furrow runs from the apex of the posterior margin of the pedicle valve, in which is the small pedicle opening. The shell ornamentation consists of concentric growth lines, and sometimes faint ribs are visible.

Size: *Orbiculoidea* grew to around 20mm (⅘in) in diameter.
Occurrence: This genus if found in strata of Ordovician to Permian age, worldwide.
Comments: As with other inarticulate brachiopods, the original shell was chitino-phosphatic.

PYGOPE

With a triangular shell outline, *Pygope* is readily recognized. The smooth shell has concentric growth lines, and a shallow groove runs centrally. Some species are almost divided in two and have distinct lobes. In the groove there is an opening through which water was squirted. Seawater entered the shell through small holes. There is a large pedicle opening, out of which the pedicle protruded, attaching the shell to the seabed.

Size: This articulate genus grew to around 80mm (3⅛in) in length.
Occurrence: From strata of Jurassic and Cretaceous age in Europe. The illustrated examples are from Verona, Italy.
Comments: *Pygope* lived in calm, deep marine conditions. The shape of the shell often changed during its life, the lobes fusing together to produce a 'keyhole' in the centre of the shell.

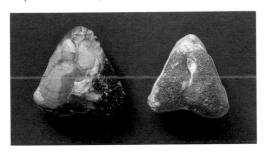

PSEUDOGLOSSOTHYRIS

An articulate brachiopod with very little shell ornamentation, *Pseudoglossothyris* has only concentric growth lines on its shell. The illustration shows the larger pedicle valve, with pedicle opening, and in front of this is the smaller brachial valve. Both valves are rounded in outline and convex. In life, this brachiopod was attached to the seabed by its pedicle, which protruded through the large pedicle opening.
Size: *Pseudoglossothyris* grew to about 100mm (4in) in length.
Occurrence: Found in Jurassic strata in Europe.
Comments: Small patches of oolitic limestone can be seen adhering to the fossil illustrated. This rock is formed in relatively

BRACHIOPODS

shallow, agitated seawater, and this gives some indication of the environment in which the brachiopod lived.

TORQUIRHYNCHIA

This genus belongs to a common group of brachiopods referred to as 'rhynchonellids', which were successful during the Mesozoic era and developed into many genera. *Torquirhynchia* is an articulate genus, with the pedicle valve slightly larger than the brachial valve. Both valves are convex and the overall shape of the shell is rounded. Thick, radiating ribs are the main ornamentation.
Size: This genus grew to around 50mm (2in) in diameter.
Occurrence: Found in rocks of Jurassic age in Europe and Russia.
Comments: *Torquirhynchia* lived in shallow marine conditions attached to the seabed.

STIPHROTHYRIS

Stiphrothyris has a relatively smooth shell, ornamented only with concentric growth lines. The large pedicle opening can be clearly seen in the illustration, and the anterior part of the shell is folded, with two smooth ridges separated by a deep sulcus. Inside the broken brachial valve, the looped brachidium is visible, coated with crystalline calcite.
Size: This articulate genus grew to around 50mm (2in) in length.
Occurrence: From Jurassic strata in Europe.
Comments: In addition to the characteristic 'rhynchonellid' brachio-

pods, another group was common during the Mesozoic era. These were 'terebratulid' types, with elongate shells similar to the one illustrated here. Many genera in this group are alive today.

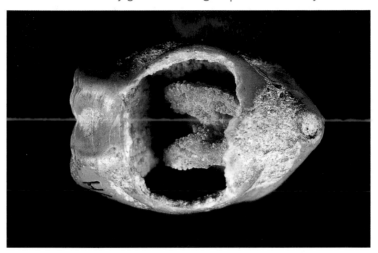

ORNITHELLA

Ornithella is another representative of the common terebratulid group. The shell outline is characteristic, being elongated, with a straight anterior margin, and widening towards the posterior end.

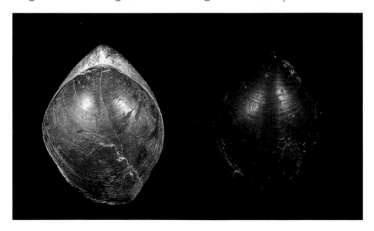

Each valve is convex, and the pedicle opening is small. The only shell ornamentation is closely spaced, concentric growth lines.

Size: This is a small articulate genus, reaching only about 25mm (1in) in length.

Occurrence: In strata of Jurassic age in Europe. *Ornithella* lived attached to the seabed in small clusters, with the pedicle valve uppermost. The pedicle was probably quite long, allowing the whole shell to be raised slightly above the seabed.

Comments: Internally, as with other terebratulid brachiopods, there is a short, looped brachidium. Different genera in this group can be distinguished not only by the external morphology but also by the size and shape of the loop.

CYCLOTHYRIS

This genus of articulate brachiopods has a characteristic triangular outline to its shell (see image on the opposite page). There is a small pedicle opening on the sharp beak. Each valve is convex, and the ornamentation consists of radiating ribs and concentric growth lines. The anterior margin of the shell has a folded, zigzag shape. This is thought to be a device to prevent relatively large particles of sediment from entering the shell when the valves were opened. It is a not uncommon feature in fossil brachiopods.

Size: A genus that reached about 25mm (1in) in width.

Occurrence: *Cyclothyris* is found in strata of Cretaceous age in North America and Europe.

Comments: It lived in small clusters attached to the seabed. Many rhynchonellid brachiopods lived in this way. The zigzag fold in the anterior of the shell is known in some Devonian brachiopods, some in the Jurassic period and in *Cyclothyris* during the Cretaceous period. It is not known in genera at other times.

TETRARHYNCHIA

Tetrarhynchia has many of the typical features of the rhynchonellid brachiopods. The small shell is covered with strong ribs, and the anterior margin is deeply folded (see image on p.108). Faint growth lines cover the convex valves. The beak is pointed, with a small pedicle opening.

Size: Usually this small brachiopod is around 25mm (1in) in diameter, though examples as large as 140mm (5⅜in) have been found.

Occurrence: From Jurassic strata in North America and Europe.

Comments: Fossils of *Tetrarhynchia* are frequently found in clusters or 'nests', in which they lived attached to the seabed. During the Jurassic period, the seabed was, at times, a shallow, hard rock surface. This may have been above sea level from time to time and therefore suffered erosion. A very varied community of organisms, including crinoids, corals, bivalve molluscs and gastropods, lived with groups of *Tetrahrynchia* on the 'hardground' when it was below sea level.

TEREBRATELLA

This terebratulid brachiopod has an oval shell with two convex valves. In the illustration, the pedicle valve can be seen behind the brachial valve (see image on the opposite page). The shell surface is ornamented with growth lines and ribs, which in some cases split in two towards the anterior shell margin. The small pedicle opening is clearly seen, as is a triangular area below it called the delthyrium, which is made of two plates.

Size: This genus grew to around 50mm (2in) in length.

Occurrence: Found worldwide in strata of Cretaceous age. The specimen is from France.

Comments: *Terebratella* lived anchored to the seabed by its fleshy pedicle.

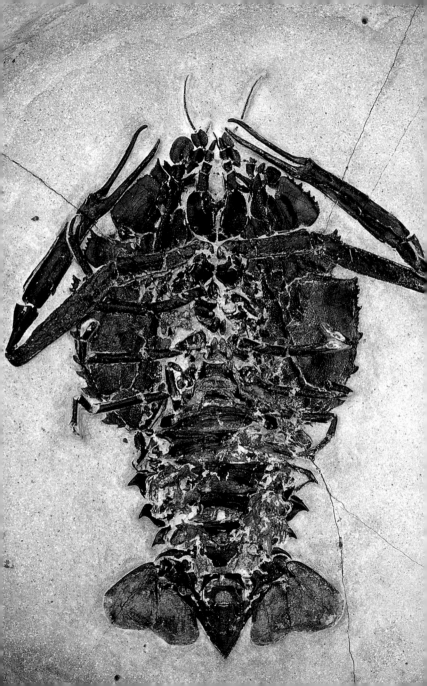

ARTHROPODS
AND GRAPTOLITES

The phylum Arthropoda is one of the most varied and successful, and includes creatures that swim in the deep ocean and in fresh water, crawl on land and even fly. Creatures as diverse as dragonflies, scorpions, lobsters and spiders are arthropods. A unifying feature is a tough, usually segmented, exoskeleton surrounding articulating sections. As the organism grows, the exoskeleton has to be repeatedly moulted by a process called ecdysis. Arthropods have a complex nervous system and brain, with body fluids circulated by a heart. Gills or a system of branching tubes (tracheae) bring air directly into the body tissue. Various appendages including legs and antennae (feelers) are present, and many arthropods have good vision. Members of the phylum are first recorded from strata of Cambrian age.

Trilobites are perhaps the best-known fossil arthropods. Their three longitudinal lobes are most obvious in the thorax, which is often the largest part of the organism, commonly having a central axis and lateral pleurae made up of small, transverse segments. The anterior cephalon (head-shield) may have compound eyes and a central glabella, which probably housed the main nervous system. A pygidium, or tail, is at the posterior end, and this typically has a similar structure to the thorax. Like other arthropods, as a trilobite grew it had to shed its exoskeleton. It is possible that any individual trilobite could leave a number of fossils; indeed, many fragmented trilobite fossils may be shed exoskeletons. Trilobites had a variety of appendages, including legs and feelers. Some undoubtedly walked on the seabed; others may have been able to swim. The segmented structure of the exoskeleton allowed the trilobite to enrol, possibly for defence. These creatures are first found in strata of Cambrian age, and became extinct in the Permian period.

OPPOSITE: **Eryon**. *This virtually perfect specimen of a fossil marine arthropod shows fine detail including the delicate feelers. It has been preserved with the carapace underneath, so all the legs and claws are visible. From Jurassic rocks near Lyme Regis, Dorset, UK.*

Other arthropods are not uncommon in the fossil record. In strata of Devonian age are found eurypterids, some of which grew to over 2m (6½ft) in length, while Carboniferous rocks contain fossilized dragonflies and spiders, some very delicate and resembling modern harvestmen. During the Mesozoic era, insects evolved rapidly. In the Jurassic rocks at Solnhofen in southern Germany, and in the Lias (Lower Jurassic) of Dorset, UK, a wealth of fossil insects has been found, including cockroaches, dragonflies, mayflies and locusts. Fossil crustaceans, such as crabs and lobsters, are well known from Mesozoic and Cenozoic strata. Arthropods also leave fossilized traces of their existence in the form of burrows and trails in and on strata, and in some cases the arthropod has been found fossilized in its burrow.

TRILOBITE STRUCTURE

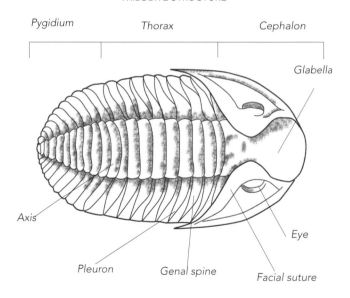

TRILOBITES

DREPANURA

Usually only the strangely shaped pygidium of this trilobite is preserved. Two are shown here, along with numerous other small fragments. The pygidium has two long, curving spines, between which are many smaller spines. *Drepanura* has a short, broad axis. In the centre of the cephalon there is a narrowing glabella with three furrows, and the eyes are at the forward margin. The thorax has thirteen spinose segments.

Size: The pygidia shown are 25mm (1in) across. The whole trilobite grew to about 50mm (2in) in length.

Occurrence: From Cambrian strata in Europe and Asia. The specimen illustrated is from China.

Comments: This trilobite has been known in the Far East for hundreds of years, and was used by Chinese alchemists.

AGNOSTUS

An easily recognized trilobite, *Agnostus* (see image on p.114) has only two thoracic segments squeezed in between the much larger cephalon and pygidium. The cephalon has a narrow glabella, which is virtually cut in half by a deep furrow. Around the margin of the cephalon is a broad, smooth border. This genus has no eyes. There is a wide border around the pygidium, and two short spines are preserved in some examples.

Size: A diminutive trilobite, *Agnostus* is usually around 10mm (⅖in) in length.

Occurrence: Found in Cambrian strata, worldwide.

Comments: Specimens from Västergötland in Sweden have been studied at high magnification and show an appendage not usually found in trilobites. This and other features of the genus may cast doubt on its classification with the trilobites. The illustration shows a mass of fossils from Västergötland.

ELLIPSOCEPHALUS

The cephalon is the widest part of the exoskeleton. It has a large, rounded glabella and rounded lateral cheeks (see image on opposite page). The margin of the cephalon is smooth, without spines. The tapering thorax has between 12 and 14 segments, and a slight groove separates the lateral segments from the thoracic axis. The pleurae divide into two near their edges.

Size: This genus grew to around 40mm (1⅜in) in length.

Occurrence: Found in Cambrian strata in North America, North Africa, Europe and Australia. The specimen illustrated is from the former Czechoslovakia. Two specimens and the impression of a third are shown.

Comments: This trilobite was first described in 1825, and so is one of the first trilobite genera recognized.

PERONOPSIS

With a similar overall structure to *Agnostus*, *Peronopsis* is easy to distinguish from other trilobites, having only two thoracic segments. These have lateral and axial structures. The cephalon has deep grooves separating the glabella from the smooth cheeks, and there is a slight groove around the margin. A furrow divides the glabella into two parts. The pygidium has a wide central axis reaching to the border.

Size: *Peronopsis* grew to around 8mm (⅓in) in length.

Occurrence: From strata of Cambrian age in North America, Europe and Siberia. The specimen illustrated is from Montana, USA.

Comments: *Peronopsis* lacks the two spines often – but not always – found on the pygidium of *Agnostus*.

ONNIA

Onnia is characterized by a large glabella with extended genal spines, which can be twice as long as the trilobite's carapace. The cephalon has a large glabella, and there are rounded cheeks on either side, without eyes. The border of the cephalon is of special interest, being made up of numerous small pits, or perforations. The short thorax has only five segments, and the axis is indistinct. A short, triangular pygidium with similar structure to the thorax is present. Often only the cephalon is found fossilized, without the long delicate spines.

Size: Onnia is a relatively small trilobite, reaching about 25mm (1in) in length.

Occurrence: Found in rocks of Ordovician age in Europe, South America and Africa. The specimen illustrated is from the Atlas Mountains of Morocco, North Africa.

Comments: The purpose of the pits around the cephalon margin is debatable. One theory holds that they were a mechanism for detecting water pressure changes or current movement.

PARADOXIDES

This large trilobite has a wide cephalon with a central, rounded glabella and crescent-shaped eyes. Long genal spines extend from the cephalon. The thorax is characterized by a typical three-fold division into central and lateral lobes. Its axis tapers posteriorly. The margins of the thorax are spinose, the spines extending and curving towards the pygidium, which is very small and rounded and often surrounded by the thoracic spines.

Size: Some individuals of this genus reach over 500mm (20in) in length. More usually specimens are around 50mm (2in) long.

Occurrence: *Paradoxides* occurs in rocks of Cambrian age in North America, South America, North Africa and Europe. *Paradoxides paradoxissimus* and *Paradoxides forchhammeri* are used as zone fossils in the Cambrian period. The specimen shown is from the former Czechoslovakia.

Comments: *Paradoxides* was one of the first trilobites to be described and named. In 1862, J.W. Salter, working for the *Geological Survey of Great Britain*, discovered the fossil of a very large trilobite near St David's in Wales, UK. It was estimated to be nearly 600mm (2ft) long. He later named it *Paradoxides davidis* after the fossil collector, David Hornfray, who provided Salter with many specimens for his research.

OLENELLUS

Olenellus is a highly spinose trilobite. The cephalon has long genal spines, with other spines extending from most of the thoracic segments. There are large, crescentric eyes on either side of the central, furrowed glabella. The thorax has fourteen segments and tapers rapidly towards the pygidium, which is small and pointed, with a tail spine.

Size: A genus that grew to around 80mm (3⅛in) in length.

Occurrence: From strata of Cambrian age in North America, Greenland and northern Scotland. The specimen illustrated is from Pennsylvania, USA.

Comments: The occurrence of *Olenellus* is of considerable importance in palaeogeographic reconstruction. Wales is a famous locality for trilobites of Cambrian age, but *Olenellus* is unknown from Welsh strata. In Britain, its only localities are in northern Scotland, especially the north-west, where in the rusty-weathering Cambrian rocks it was first discovered in the early years of the 20th century. Along with other evidence, the distribution of *Olenellus* suggests that a wide, deep ocean, across which this trilobite could not migrate, separated Wales from another landmass on which North America and Scotland were situated during Cambrian times.

OGYGOPSIS

Ogygopsis has a relatively small cephalon containing a glabella with eyes on its edges (see image on the opposite page). Genal spines run from the edge of the cephalon. The thorax has eight

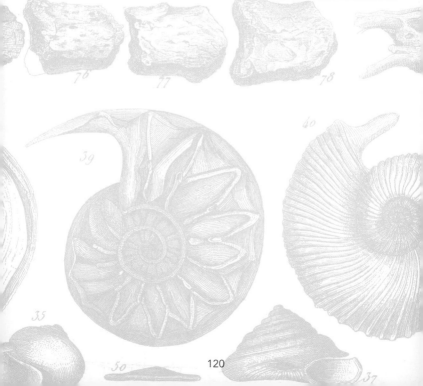

THE BURGESS SHALE

High in the Rocky Mountains of British Columbia lies one of the most famous fossil localities. Here, thousands of metres above sea level, is hardened mud from the Cambrian seabed containing fossils of rarely preserved, soft-bodied creatures such as jellyfish and worms. It was the chance find of a perfect trilobite in 1909 by Charles Walcott that led him back there in 1917 with a collecting team that found over 40,000 fossils. The unshelled organisms had probably been engulfed in mud slides falling from a submarine reef, and this soft sediment was able to preserve their delicate details. A great variety of different creatures are found fossilized together, and this backs up the mud slide theory, as they would not all have lived in the same part of the seabed. It is possible that this rare case of fossilization gives us a glimpse of a fairly typical Cambrian fauna.

segments, and the pleurae have short spines pointing towards the pygidium, which is longer than the cephalon and has a narrow, convex border. Down the centre of the thorax is an axis, which tapers through to the pygidium.

Size: This genus grew to around 100mm (4in) in length.

Occurrence: In Cambrian strata in North America. The specimen illustrated is from the Burgess Shale of British Columbia, Canada.

ASAPHUS

This genus shows the typical trilobite structure of three lengthwise lobes. It is also clearly divided into cephalon, thorax and pygidium. The cephalon is triangular in shape, and the genal angles, where the cephalon meets the thorax, are rounded and spineless. The central glabella, which has large eyes, reaches the edge of the

carapace. There is no border on the cephalon. Wide, articulating segments make up the thorax, and the pleural lobes have sharp ridges. The pygidium has a long axis and indistinct pleurae.

Size: This genus grew to around 80mm (3⅛in) in length.

Occurrence: From Ordovician strata in north-west Europe and Russia. The specimen shown is from Russia.

Comments: *Asaphus* may have lived on the seabed, partly covered with sediment, with its large eyes protruding.

OGYGINUS

The thorax, cephalon and pygidium of *Ogyginus* are about the same size. The cephalon has a distinct glabella with large eyes on either side, and there is an obvious facial suture running from each eye towards the thorax. Genal spines extend along the sides of the thorax to about the midpoint, and the cephalon has a wide border. There are eight thoracic segments. The segmentation of the pygidium is less distinct than that of the thorax. The axis has a rounded

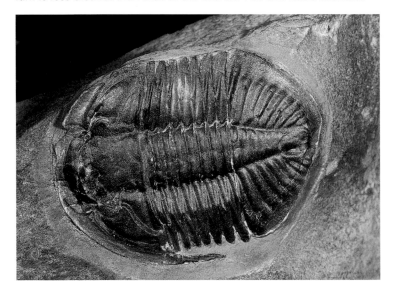

termination short of the margin of the carapace.
Size: This genus grew to about 50mm (2in) in length.
Occurrence: From strata of Ordovician age in Europe. The specimen shown is from Builth Wells, Wales, UK.
Comments: This trilobite probably had good vision. The facial suture, seen in the illustrated specimen, is where the carapace split to allow moulting.

TRIARTHRUS

Triarthrus has a rounded, semi-circular cephalon and a furrowed glabella with eyes on the margin. There are 12 to 16 thoracic seg-

ments, and the axis reaches into the small, triangular pygidium.

Size: *Triarthrus* grew to around 30mm (1⅛in) in length.

Occurrence: From Ordovician rocks, worldwide. The specimen illustrated is from New York, USA.

Comments: This genus is of great interest because specimens from Ordovician black shales in New York have been preserved with limbs, feelers and other appendages. There are two feelers, rather like modern arthropods' antennae. Some of the limbs are jointed and branched, and have fringes with thin filaments on them. Most of the appendages reach out beyond the margin of the carapace. The limbs may be for walking on the seabed or for swimming slightly above it.

ACIDASPIS

Acidaspis is characterized by its spinose carapace. The cephalon has spines along its front margin, and there are eyes beside the glabella (see image on p.124). Genal spines reach to the sixth thoracic segment. The thorax has long, curved spines extending from each pleural segment. The indistinct axis tapers to the border with the pygidium, which is rather like a small comb, having four small spines and two longer marginal spines.

Size: This small trilobite grew to around 25mm (1in) in length.

Occurrence: Found in Ordovician, Silurian and Devonian rocks in North America and Europe.

Comments: The spines on the carapace of this genus may have allowed the trilobite to support itself just above the seabed.

TRINUCLEUS

The cephalon of *Trinucleus* is large and far wider than the rest of the exoskeleton (see image on the opposite page). There is a rounded glabella, which has small indentations along its margins. Eyes are absent. The margin of the cephalon is characterized by a wide, flattened border containing elongated pits, which radiate around the cephalon. Detailed studies have shown that these pits are linked by a tiny canal. Their exact purpose is unknown, but it has been suggested that they may have been able to detect differences in water pressure. Long genal spines, missing in this specimen, could extend beyond the margin of the thorax, which has a narrow, central axial lobe and wide lateral lobes. There are six thoracic segments. The pygidium is similar in structure to the thorax, and is triangular in outline.

Size: *Trinucleus* was a small trilobite, growing to only 30mm (1⅛in).

Occurrence: This genus can be found in Ordovician strata in Britain and Russia. The specimen is from Wales, UK.

Comments: *Trinucleus* is often found in strata formed in deep marine conditions with other trilobites and the brachiopod *Lingulella*. It has been described as a 'mud-grubbing' trilobite, and a theory about the fringe on the cephalon is that it acted as a shovelling device for pushing through seabed sediment.

CROMUS

This small trilobite is characterized by a cephalon covered with small tubercles. The glabella, which is cut by four pairs of lateral furrows, becomes wider towards the anterior border. Eyes are present on the margins of the glabella. Ten segments make up the thorax, and this also has a pustulated surface. A slight groove runs down the centre of the axis in both the thorax and pygidium. This rapidly narrows and terminates in a small, oval structure.

Size: The genus grew up to about 25mm (1in) in length.
Occurrence: From strata of Silurian age in Europe, Australia and Africa.
Comments: It is thought that Cromus lived on or near the seabed and sifted through unconsolidated sediment.

BUMASTUS

Unlike many other trilobites, *Bumastus* has a smooth cephalon and pygidium. These are of similar size. No obvious glabella is present. Large eyes, which are difficult to distinguish on many fossils, are present on the margins of the cephalon. The thorax lacks the usual trilobite three-lobed structure, having narrow segments that cross the entire thorax. There are usually ten of these.
Size: This genus grew to around 100mm (4in) in length.

126

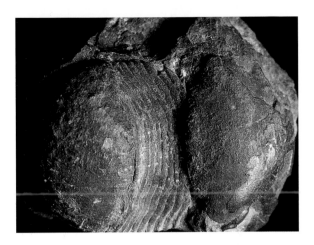

Occurrence. Found in strata of Silurian age in North America and Europe.
Comments: It has been suggested that this style of carapace is not well suited to swimming or crawling. *Bumastus* probably lived on the sea-bed, possibly burrowing in sediment.

DALMANITES
A well-known genus, *Dalmanites* has a typical trilobite appearance, with a cephalon that has rounded margins. A short spine growing from the centre of the border is present in many fossils. The glabella widens towards the anterior margin of the cephalon, and there are large, crescent-shaped eyes, which may have given good vision

through a wide angle. The thorax has 11 segments, and the pleural lobes curve towards the pygidium at their margins. The small, triangular pygidium may have a long spine extending from it.

Size: *Dalmanites* grew to about 100mm (4in) in length.

Occurrence: In strata of Silurian and Devonian age in North America, Europe, Russia and Australia.

Comments: This trilobite is often found fossilized in limestones formed in shallow reef environments. Other fossils here include corals, brachiopods and molluscs. Because the large eyes were raised above the cephalon, it may have been able to live slightly buried in seabed sediment.

PHACOPS

This genus has a large cephalon, which contains a glabella ornamented with tubercles. Analogy with modern arthropods suggests that these may have had a sensory function. In *Phacops*, the tubercles have small, rounded cavities below them from which slender canals radiate. There are large eyes on the sides of the cephalon. The genal angle is rounded and lacks spines. The thorax consists of

11 segments, and the central axis tapers through to the posterior end of the pygidium.

Size: This genus grew to around 150mm (6in) in length.

Occurrence: *Phacops* is found in strata of Silurian and Devonian age in North America, North Africa and Europe.

Comments: This genus is often found enrolled. Fossils from North Germany have been preserved with legs and other appendages.

SCUTELLUM

This is an unusual trilobite for a number of reasons, particularly the structure of the pygidium. From the point where this joins the thorax, a number of ribs radiate across the pygidium. The thorax in *Scutellum* has ten segments. The central axial lobe is wider than the pleural

TRILOBITE EYES

Because trilobite eyes are made of calcite, they are often well preserved in fossils. They have compound lenses, with many small, rounded or polygonal lenses being joined in each eye. Calcite has been shown to have excellent optical properties; light will pass through it in certain directions as perfectly as through glass. Most trilobites have what are called holochral eyes, in which there may be thousands of individual lenses all joined by a single covering of cornea. A more advanced system is found in the group of trilobites called the phacopids. This is the only  group to have schizochral eyes, which today are unknown. In these eyes the lenses are arranged with cuticle between them, and a separate piece of cornea lies on each lens. Research has shown that this type of lens gives a sharply focused image. What quality of vision trilobites had is unknown. Compound eyes in modern arthropods are excellent for detecting movement, and so useful for both food-collecting and sensing danger.

lobes, which have narrow spines extending from them. The cephalon is smaller than the pygidium, and has a small, raised glabella.
Size: This genus grew to about 90mm (3⅜in).
Occurrence: *Scutellum* occurs in strata of Silurian and Devonian age, worldwide. The specimen is from Devonian rocks in Morocco.
Comments: This trilobite's eyes are very complex, having over 4,000 individual lenses. It could probably have detected movement of small objects, and may have had good vision in dark conditions.

TRIMERUS

Most trilobites have a thorax divided longitudinally into three lobes, a narrow central lobe and two broader lateral lobes. In *Trimerus* the thorax is segmented, but the division into lobes is absent. The cephalon, not seen in this specimen, is triangular in shape, but eyes are lacking. The glabella is only poorly developed as a slightly raised area in the cephalon. The pygidium is more typical. It is triangular, and is divided into axial and lateral lobes, with segmentation.

Size: This genus grew to around 200mm (8in) in length.
Occurrence: This trilobite occurs in strata of Silurian and Devonian age, worldwide. The specimen is from Shropshire, UK.
Comments: It has been suggested that, because the exoskeleton is so smooth and there are no eyes, *Trimerus* may have burrowed into the seabed sediment.

DECHENELLA

Dechenella has a broad border to the cephalon, and long, wide genal spines, extending most of the distance along the thorax.

There are large eyes beside the furrowed glabella, which tapers anteriorly. The thoracic axis is pronounced, and has strong segmentation, as do the lateral lobes of the thorax. The pygidium is long, with a definite border.

Size: This genus grew to around 50mm (2in) in length.

Occurrence: From Devonian strata in the Northern Hemisphere. The example illustrated is from Morocco.

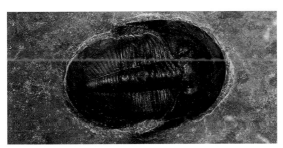

Comments: *Dechenella* is thought to have lived on the seabed, probably sifting sediment for food.

REEDOPS

This trilobite is related to *Phacops*, and has some similar features. Overall, the carapace is slender. The cephalon contains a smooth glabella, unlike *Phacops*, which has a glabella covered in tubercles. The front lobe of the glabella reaches beyond the margin of the cephalon, on which are large eyes. The thorax has marked furrows and segmentation, which is less obvious on the pygidium. This has a smooth, rounded margin.

Size: The genus grew to about 25mm (1in) in length.

Occurrence: Found in Devonian strata in North America, North Africa, Asia and Europe. The specimen illustrated is from Morocco.
Comments: *Reedops* probably lived in quite deep marine conditions, scavenging on the seabed.

CALYMENE

The cephalon is nearly triangular, with a large, central glabella, on each side of which are two rounded, knob-like protrusions. A deep groove surrounds the glabella. The rather pointed posterior ends of the cephalon mark the widest part of the exoskeleton. The thorax, clearly divided into axial and pleural lobes, has 12 or 13 segments, and tapers slightly towards the pygidium, which is very similar to the thorax, and has six segments (see image on the opposite page).
Size: *Calymene* grew to a maximum length of 100mm (4in).
Occurrence: Found in Silurian and Devonian strata in Europe, Australia, North America and South America. The specimen shown is from Shropshire, UK.
Comments: In strata from Cincinnati, USA, specimens of *Calymene* have been found with their carapaces resting in small, excavated grooves. These may be fossilized trails left in seabed sediment by the moving trilobites.

ENROLLING IN TRILOBITES

Both *Calymene* and *Flexicalymens* (shown here, enrolled) have often been found in an enrolled condition. Other trilobites also occur like this – indeed, some genera are able to link the pygidium and cephalon together by small extensions on the exoskeleton. Modern arthropods such as pillbugs are able to enroll with the tough exoskeleton outermost. The precise reason for trilobite enrolling is uncertain, but there are a number of possibilities. As a defensive posture, enrolling would serve to protect the soft tissues on the ventral surface. It has also been suggested that by adopting an enrolled position, a trilobite would have been able to conserve energy and rest when food was scarce; it may have remained like this for some time.

OTHER ARTHROPODS

EUESTHERIA

This small 'shelled' organism is part of the class Branchiopoda (branchiopods), a group including waterfleas and related creatures. These bivalved organisms resemble small bivalve molluscs, but the carapace is made of chitin. The internal structure is also very different from that of a mollusc shell, as *Euestheria* does not have the muscle scars familiar in bivalve mollusc shells. Also, branchiopods have limbs and other appendages, typical of an arthropod. The carapaces of *Euestheria* have concentric growth lines, which are formed during ecdysis (moulting).

Size: This genus grows to only 20mm (⅘in).

Occurrence: In strata ranging from Devonian to Recent age, worldwide. The illustration shows numerous carapaces, and is from Jurassic rocks on the Isle of Skye, Scotland, UK.

Comments: Today, organisms related to *Euestheria* live in freshwater lakes, for example, in South Africa. The occurrence of these fossils may indicate a similar environment in the past.

GLYPHEA

This arthropod is classified in the order Decapoda (decapods), which includes familiar creatures such as lobsters, prawns and shrimps. As the name of the order suggests, these organisms have five pairs of limbs, which may be adapted for either swimming or walking. *Glyphea* is rarely found fossilized with these limbs. This

genus has a rough-textured exoskeleton covered in small, rounded depressions. The remains of the appendages protruding from the head are visible. In life, these would have been feelers. Eyes with good vision were also present.

Size: The genus grew to around 50mm (2in) in length.

Occurrence: Found in strata of Triassic, Jurassic and Cretaceous age in North America, Europe, East Africa, Australia and Greenland.

Comments: Sometimes *Glyphea* can be found fossilized in its seabed burrow.

AEGER

Aeger belongs to the order Decapoda, and, though the genus is extinct, it has many similarities to modern shrimps and prawns.

There is a delicate segmented carapace, which, as the illustration shows, was flexible. At the posterior end there is a small, 'feathered' tail. The head has a large, beak-like projection on its upper surface that extends forward above the antennae. The legs and other appendages have been preserved in this fossil, and show the typical arthropod segmented structure. Some of these appendages were adapted for swimming, others for holding food.

Size: This genus grew to around 100mm (4in) in length.

Occurrence: *Aeger* is found in rocks of Triassic and Jurassic age, worldwide.

Comments: Even though this arthropod has a delicate, thin carapace, originally made of both chitin and calcium carbonate, it is well known in certain parts of the fossil record. The specimen illustrated is from the famous Solnhofen limestones in Southern Germany. In these exceptionally fine-grained limestones, many delicate organisms, such as jellyfish, worms and insects, have been fossilized. These rocks, the 'Plattenkalk', were formed in a lagoon, separated from the open sea by a reef or sand bar. This was not a good habitat because of the high salinity and temperature of the water, and most of the fossils found in the limestone were washed in by storms or rivers.

MESOLIMULUS

The carapace of *Mesolimulus* has a large, semi-circular cephalon, with a wide border and very short genal spines (see image on the opposite page). The compound eyes, placed towards the sides of the cephalon, are kidney-shaped. The short thorax has a marked central axis, six pairs of lateral spines, and five pairs of legs. Also, there is a pair of pincers at the anterior end of the thorax. A long, slender tail spine extends from the small pygidium.

Size: This genus grew to as much as 250mm (10in) in length.

Occurrence: From strata of Triassic, Jurassic and Cretaceous age in Europe. The illustrated example is from the famous Solnhofen limestone.

Comments: This fossil king crab bears a striking resemblance to modern forms, which today live on the coast of South-East Asia, around the Indian Ocean and on the Atlantic coast of North America.

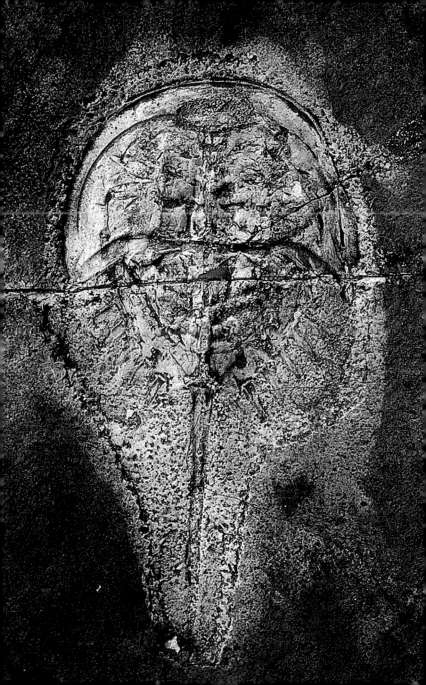

PTERYGOTUS

Pterygotus is classified as a member of the subclass Eurypterida (eurypterids). These arthropods have a relatively small head, from which extend long claws, used for grabbing their prey. There are six pairs of limb-like appendages. The large posterior pair, which are paddle-shaped, were probably used for moving about on the seabed or in the water. At the anterior end of the head are a pair of antennae, and the remaining four pairs of appendages may well have been for feeding. Compound eyes are located on the upper surface of the head-shield near the anterior margin. The long, tapering thorax has 12 segments, and at the posterior end is a spiked tail.

Size: Most specimens are small, but *Pterygotus* could grow to 2m (78in) in length, the biggest arthropods known.

Occurrence: Found in strata of Ordovician, Silurian and Devonian age in North America, South America, Australia, Asia and Europe.

Comments: Eurypterids such as *Pterygotus* are thought to have been fierce predators on the Palaeozoic seabed. The genus probably fed on fishes, which were evolving rapidly during the Devonian period, and on molluscs and other invertebrates.

EUPHORBERIA

The long, segmented body of this genus of arthropods resembles that of modern millipedes and centipedes. It is classified with them in the superclass Myrapoda. The many slender appendages can be seen in the specimen. *Euphorberia* has a head wider than its body, which bears spines as well as legs.

Size: The genus grew to around 80mm (3⅛in) in length.

Occurrence: In non-marine strata of Carboniferous age in North America and Europe.

Comments: Fossil millipedes are known from rocks as old as Silurian age. This example, preserved in a hard nodule, is from Carboniferous strata in Staffordshire, UK. Such organisms were probably common in the swamp forests that flourished on the vast Carboniferous deltas, along with many insects and other invertebrates. It is unusual to find delicate, land-dwelling organisms in the fossil record, as they are less likely to become trapped in sediment than creatures living in the sea.

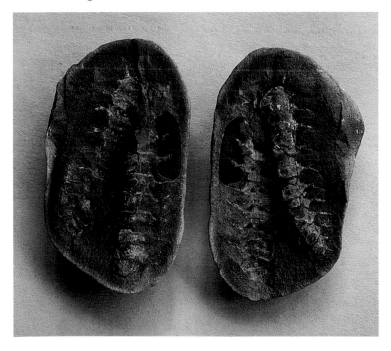

INSECTS IN THE FOSSIL RECORD

For many reasons, it is remarkable that insects are found in reasonable abundance in the fossil record. They are delicate organisms, with easily broken exoskeletons, wings and append-ages. Insects live on land or in the air, so stand only a relatively low chance of being covered in sediment and fossilized. How-ever, the exoskeleton of most insects is very durable, and even the transparent, beautifully veined wings of dragonflies are occasionally preserved in fine-grained sediments. Amber (p.48) has been responsible for the perfect preservation of a number of insect genera. Claims of insect DNA being recovered from such material are probably unfounded, as DNA decays very rapidly. The earliest insects appeared in the Devonian period, where their fossil remains occur in the famous Rhynie chert in Scotland, probably a peat deposit replaced by silica. During the Carboniferous period, winged insects flourished, with large dragonflies hawking through the coal-measure forests. By the close of Palaeozoic time, many insects had adopted the well-documented life cycle of egg, larva, pupa and adult. During the Mesozoic era, many modern insects evolved, in-cluding wasps, earwigs, fleas, ants and termites. Then, and into the Cenozoic era, the flowering plants were colouring the land surface and producing nectar and pollen. They evolved along-side butterflies, bees and other nectar- and pollen-feeding insects, which provided a means of fertilizing the flowers. Many new fossil insects have lately come to light in recently explored areas, such as Brazil, parts of Russia, China and Mongolia.

FAR LEFT: Mayfly (specimen of Cretaceous age, from Brazil).
LEFT: Bee (specimen from Cenozoic of France).
ABOVE: Beetle Cybister (specimen from Pleistocene of California, USA).
BELOW: Amber with gnat (specimen from Baltic region).

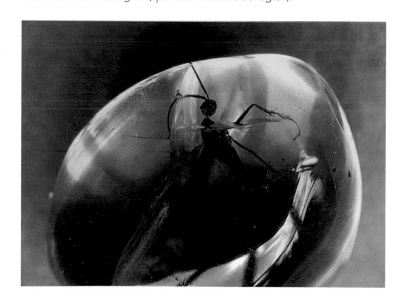

GRAPTOLITES

The enigmatic graptolites are usually classified in a group of their own – phylum Hemichordata. That they were marine organisms is without doubt, as their fossils are found in sedimentary rocks formed in deep-sea conditions, ranging in age from Cambrian to Devonian. The graptolite has a stick-like structure called a stipe, on which there are small cups or thecae; in each of these lived a zooid. There is a tremendous variety of stipes in the different genera. Most graptolites are small and delicate, and are usually preserved as flattened traces of carbon or pyrite in fine-grained sediments. However, three-dimensional fossils, like those from glacial erratics in North Germany, can be removed by dissolving the rock in acid.

The use of electron microscopes has enabled the detailed structure of the stipes and thecae of some species of graptolite to be investigated, and it seems that collagen is a major component. This formed as bandage-like layers, giving the stipe strength. Individual species of graptolites are found over a wide geographical area, and so are useful as zone fossils. Two main groups are distinguished: the dendroid graptolites have numerous interconnected stipes, giving a tree-like appearance, while the graptoloid graptolites have fewer stipes, sometimes only one.

GRAPTOLITE STRUCTURE

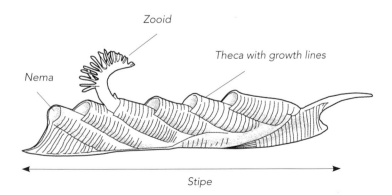

Zooid

Theca with growth lines

Nema

Stipe

PHYLLOGRAPTUS

This graptoloid graptolite has stipes that rather resemble leaves.
The whole structure consists of four stipes joined 'back to back'
to give a cross-shaped section. When fossilized, the structure is
invariably crushed, so that, as in the illustration, only two stipes can
be seen. The thecae are simple and tube-shaped, and vary with
different species, some being curved, others toothed.

Size: A small graptolite, usually around 25mm (1in) in length.
Occurrence: In strata of Ordovician age, worldwide. The specimen
shown is from Norway.
Comments: This genus was probably planktonic, being carried by
ocean currents.

MONOGRAPTUS

Because the thecae are on only one side of the single stipe,
Monograptus is described as a uniserial graptolite. There are a
number of species within this genus, differing in the shape and
arrangement of the thecae, some being hook-shaped, others
curved. The stipe, though usually straight, can be coiled.
Size: Stipes are commonly about 25mm (1in) long, but may be over
500mm (20in) long.

Occurrence: From Silurian and Devonian rocks in North America and Europe.
Comments: Some *Monograptus* species are used as zone fossils for Silurian rocks.

DIDYMOGRAPTUS

This genus is easily recognized by the two stipes joined in a 'V' shape, rather like a tuning fork. In some species the stipes are at a narrow angle to each other, while others are virtually at 180°. The stipes have thecae on only one side, and so are uniserial. The thecae vary from species to species, and can be simple tubes, hook-shaped or curved.

Size: Usually this graptolite is around 25mm (1in) in length, but some specimens are as much as 500mm (20in) long

Occurrence: A common genus in strata of Ordovician age, worldwide.

Comments: Often found in great numbers on bedding planes, *Didymograptus* may well have been planktonic and drifted on ocean currents. Rocks of Ordovician age are subdivided into zones using this graptolite.

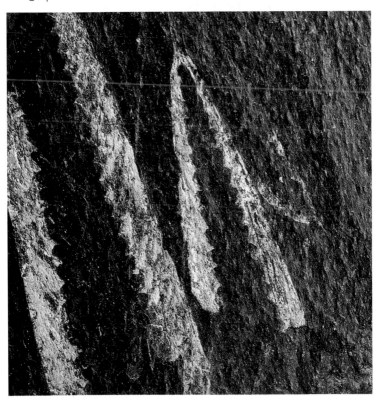

DICTYONEMA

This dendroid graptolite has a rather different structure from that of the graptoloids. There are numerous thin stipes joined by transverse bars (see the image on the opposite page). The small thecae are numerous and constructed in groups of three, but are only on one side of each stipe. A typical fossil of *Dictyonema* has the appearance of a flattened, net-like bag, which tapers at one end. There is much debate as to how this genus lived. The graptolites could have been attached to algae or the seabed, and some may have floated as plankton.

Size: The genus ranges from about 25–250mm (1–10in) in length.

Occurrence: In strata from Cambrian to Carboniferous age, worldwide.

Comments: The possible planktonic life-style of *Dictyonema* may be suggested by its wide distribution and the fact that it is one of the small number of Ordovician fossils found in both Western Europe and North America. These areas were separated by a wide ocean at this time.

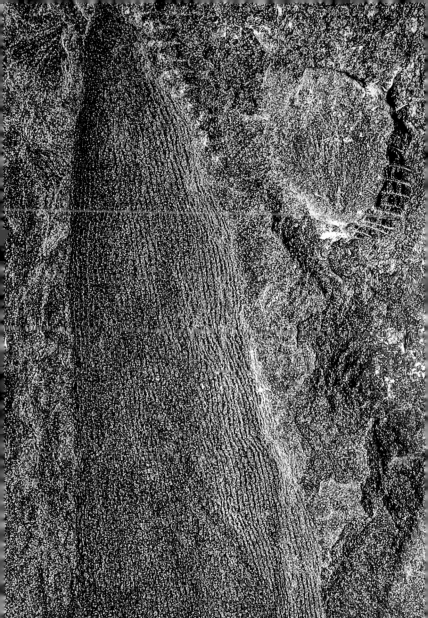

MOLLUSCS

The first fossil molluscs occur in Cambrian rocks, and they have become one of the most diverse phyla. Their Pre-Cambrian ancestors are unknown, but may have been soft-bodied, segmented creatures or something resembling the modern *Neopilina*. This creature is a monoplacophoran, believed extinct until about 50 years ago, when living specimens were found off Mexico and Peru. Monoplacophorans have a limpet-like shell, beneath which lies a molluscan body, with a foot and gills. Typical molluscs have a soft mantle surrounding their body; this may be enclosed in a shell, or supported internally. Molluscs are adapted to various habitats; many are marine, others live in fresh water, and some live on dry land, even climbing rock faces and trees.

There are a number of classes within the phylum. Three are important in the fossil record. The gastropods (class Gastropoda) include the well-known snails and slugs. Marine gastropods, and some from fresh water, are common fossils. The gastropod shell is either coiled in a spiral or cone-shaped, and is usually composed of aragonite, a form of calcium carbonate. The coiled type of shell can be complex. Internally, there is a central columella supporting the hollow structure. The coils, called whorls, vary in number and size with genera, but the largest whorl is where the animal lived, extending its body through the aperture. Often there is a fleshy foot, a head with eyes and tentacles, and, in some genera, an operculum for closing the aperture of the shell.

The bivalves (class Bivalvia) are two-shelled molluscs, usually with a plane of symmetry between the valves. They are the clams, scallops and tellins well known to beachcombers. Typically the valves are mirror images of each other (but some bivalves, including the oysters, have different symmetry), and on the outside may have growth lines, ribs, nodes and spines. The two valves are joined along a hinge line just below the umbo, a beak-like projection on

OPPOSITE: **Xiphoceras** *and other ammonites. Ammonite shells often accumulated in numbers on the Jurassic seabed. This mass was surrounded by dark mud, now shale, and thus preserved intact. The specimen shown is from Dorset, UK.*

each valve. A system of teeth in one valve and matching sockets in the other acts as a hinge mechanism, together with horny ligament. Muscles inside the shell hold the valves together, and if relaxed, the shell is pulled fractionally open by the ligament. When a bivalve dies and the muscles relax, the valves fall apart, and single valves are common as fossils.

Cephalopods (class Cephalopoda) are the fossil goniatites and ammonites (which make up the subclass Ammonoidea), nautiloids and belemnites. Today, the class is less diverse and includes the pearly nautilus, octopods and squids. The cephalopods are marine creatures, usually with a shell that has buoyancy chambers allowing them to live above the seabed. These chambers are interconnected by a narrow tube, the siphuncle, and so buoyancy can be varied. In the ammonites and goniatites the siphuncle is ventral, but the nautiloid shell has a central siphuncle. Most of these cephalopods have a shell coiled in a flat plane, with a depression called the umbilicus often situated deeply in the middle. An important feature of the complex shell architecture is the septa, which divide the chambers from one another. Where these meet the inner surface of the shell, there are suture lines, very elaborate in the ammonites. The ammonite body was like that of a squid, and lived in the first part of the shell, the body chamber, in front of the buoyancy chambers. Ammonites could move by jet propulsion, but many of the larger ones probably lived near the seabed. Squids have an internal, calcareous shell, and the belemnites, many of which lived at the same time as the ammonites, had such an internal shell, often found fossilized. It consists of a pointed, bullet-shaped guard, with a chambered phragmacone fitting into the wider end. These two parts are often found separately as fossils.

GASTROPOD STRUCTURE

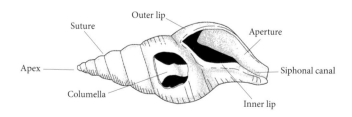

BIVALVE STRUCTURE

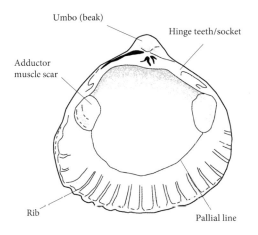

Internal
view

Umbo (beak)

Hinge teeth/socket

Adductor
muscle scar

Rib

Pallial line

AMMONOID STRUCTURE

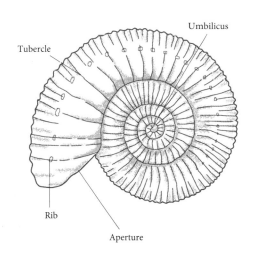

External
view

Umbilicus

Tubercle

Rib

Aperture

GASTROPODS

BELLEROPHON

This sea snail is recognized by the keel that runs around the shell and the many ribs that cross the keel. The opening of the shell (the aperture) has a wide, flared edge with a pronounced exhalant slit at the front. The overall structure is unlike that of many gastropods because it has bilateral symmetry. The outermost whorl envelops the inner whorls as in a cephalopod shell. However, it is easy to distinguish *Bellerophon* from an ammonite or other cephalopod, because these have internal septa and suture lines, while the gastropod lacks these features.

Size: *Bellerophon* reached around 100mm (4in) in diameter.

Occurrence: This gastropod is found in strata ranging in age from Silurian to Triassic, worldwide. Carboniferous genera are often found in limestones deposited in shallow marine reefs, with brachiopods, other molluscs, algae and corals.

Comments: *Bellerophon* is of some historic importance, as in 1808 the genus was the first mollusc from Palaeozoic rocks to be scientifically described. It belongs to a group referred to as the Bellerophontaceans, which contains around 70 genera.

STRAPAROLLUS

Unlike *Bellerophon*, this genus has a more typical gastropod shell that is spirally coiled. In some species of the genus the shell forms a much taller spiral than in the one illustrated. The coiling is such that the inner whorls can be seen. The shell surface is generally smooth, with very fine ribs running across the whorls. A broad but indistinct ridge runs around the centre of each whorl.

Size: This genus grew to around 50mm (2in) in diameter.

Occurrence: In strata ranging from Silurian to Permian age, worldwide. The specimen is from rocks of Carboniferous age, in Derbyshire, UK.

Comments: *Straparollus* is found with fossils of other shallow-water organisms such as corals, brachiopods and algae. It probably browsed on algae and seabed detritus.

TENTACULITES

This somewhat enigmatic fossil is often found in great numbers, crowding bedding planes (see image on p.154). *Tentaculites* has a shell made originally of calcite, which forms a slender tube or cone. This is ornamented with thick ridges, and internally it is subdivided by septa. It has been suggested that the strong ridges running around the shell helped to anchor it into soft seabed sediment.

MOLLUSCS

Size: A small fossil only about 12mm (½in) in length.

Occurrence: In strata of Silurian and Devonian age, worldwide. Usually it is fossilized in shallow-water sedimentary rocks, like the Silurian limestone of Ravena, New York, USA, and the Ordovician continental shelf deposits in Wales, UK.

Comments: From its structure, *Tentaculites* is generally assigned to the phylum Mollusca. It probably has greater affinities with modern pelagic and planktonic gastropods than with other groups. However, some fossil material, in which soft parts can be studied, suggests this genus may have features, such as a siphuncle, which link these organisms to the Cephalopoda.

MOURLONIA

This genus has a shell that coils in a clockwise direction when viewed from above (see image on the opposite page above). The individual whorls do not overlap very much, and the suture between the whorls is delicate. Shell ornamentation consists of numerous thin bands running across each whorl and curving away from the aperture, which is relatively large.

Size: *Mourlonia* grew to about 40mm (1⅜in) in diameter.

Occurrence: From strata of Ordovician to Permian age, worldwide.

Comments: *Mourlonia* is found in rocks that are consistent with shallow marine deposition. It occurs in reef deposits with brachiopods and other molluscs and with bryozoans, which, because of their net-like structure, helped to bind the reef sediment together.

HIPPOCHRENES

This rather unusual gastropod is characterized by the flared extension to the shell, which develops as a flattened area above the aperture and is ornamented with concentric growth lines, forming small ridges. The shell is pointed at both ends, and tapers to a

spire. In some species the apex of the shell is obscured, at least in part, by the shell extension. In others the extension only reaches part of the way up the spire. There is a long canal in the lower part of the large body whorl.

MOLLUSCS

Size: *Hippochrenes* grew to around 150mm (6in) in length.
Occurrence: Found in strata of Eocene age in Europe.
Comments: This gastropod is found fossilized with many other molluscs that are all characteristic of shallow marine conditions.

PLEUROTOMARIA

Pleurotomaria has a shell that coils, with slight asymmetry, in a clockwise direction into a low spire. The whorls gradually narrow from the large aperture towards the apex. On the outer lip of the large aperture there is a slit, which develops, as the shell grows,

into a spiral band. Ornamentation consists of growth lines, tubercles and low ridges.
Size: This genus grew to around 120mm (4⅘in) in diameter.
Occurrence: Found in strata of Jurassic and Cretaceous age, worldwide. It is interesting to note that the larger group to which *Pleurotomaria* belongs was common until the end of the Cretaceous period and then declined, until today gastropods in this group are known only in the seas around Japan and the East and West Indies.
Comments: This well-known genus occurs with ammonites, brachiopods and bivalve molluscs, usually in rocks deposited in shallow marine conditions. It probably browsed on the seabed, feeding on algae.

TURRITELLA

This gastropod is easily recognized by the screw-shaped shell. Indeed, modern species are given names such as the 'tower screw shell' and 'European screw shell'. *Turritella* has a long, slender shell

made of many small whorls that overlap only slightly, with a pronounced suture between them. The spire is a delicate point, while at the wide end the aperture is squarish. There are growth lines and spiral markings on the outer surface.

Size: This genus can grow up to 100mm (4in) in length.

Occurrence: *Turritella* is found in strata of Cretaceous to Recent age, worldwide.

Comments: Often fossilized in great numbers, this gastropod occurs in shallow-water sedimentary rocks along with other molluscs, corals, fishes and crustaceans. Modern species burrow into soft, seabed sediment, with the apex of the shell downwards and the aperture just at the surface.

CORNULINA

Cornulina has an elaborate shell with a delicate apex, but it widens rapidly to a very large body whorl. There is a shoulder on each whorl where it meets the successive one. The stout shell is covered with thin bands and large spines, which are often broken in fossil specimens. The edge of the aperture is wide and flared.

Size: This genus reached around 100mm (4in) in diameter.

Occurrence: In rocks of Eocene to Recent age, worldwide.

MOLLUSCS

Comments: *Cornulina* is one of the many molluscs and other fossils from the famous Barton Beds of Eocene age, found in Hampshire, UK. By analogy with modern relatives of this fauna, it is suggested that the sea temperature was around 18°C (64°F) or more, and the depth of water up to 50m (164ft).

PLANORBIS

This gastropod shell is coiled in a flat spiral. The shell is different on both sides, the ventral surface being concave and the other surface flat. *Planorbis* has a very thin shell and lacks a spire, the central depression taking its place. The whorls widen considerably towards the aperture, with a deep suture running between them. Depending on species, the aperture may be oval or crescentric. Very little ornamentation covers the shell surface; there can be faint growth lines.
Size: This genus grows to around 40mm (1⅜in) in diameter.

Occurrence: *Planorbis* is found in rocks of Oligocene to Recent age, worldwide.

Comments: The thin shell is typical of a mollusc living in fresh water, where there is less calcium carbonate available for shell construction than in the sea. Modern species occur in both still and running water, feeding on algae. Some species can tolerate very poor water conditions in which oxygen is scarce. They are able to store oxygen in haemoglobin to counter such an environment, and may at times breathe air at the surface.

MUREX

This is a very varied genus. Some species are large and very spinose, others smaller. In a number of modern species there is a very long extension of the shell, rather like a 'tail', which incorporates the siphonal canal. Some of the variation is shown in the illustration. *Murex* has a thick shell with few whorls. The body whorl is far larger than the others, which form the short spire. There are strong growth lines, and a variety of ornamentation, including spines and ridges, adorns the shell. The aperture is usually large with an extension.

Size: This varies considerably with different species: some grow to 100mm (4in) in length.
Occurrence: Found in strata of Miocene to Recent age, worldwide.
Comments: This gastropod is a carnivore. The sexes usually only live together when mating. *Murex* lives in shallow marine conditions today; more species are found in warmer waters.

GALBA

This delicate shell is recognized by its tapering shape and large body whorl. There is a simple aperture. Each whorl is ornamented with delicate growth lines, and a moderately deep suture marks the point where the whorls join.
Size: The genus grows to around 70mm (2⅘in) in length.

Occurrence: Found in strata of Jurassic to Recent age in Europe.
Comments: *Galba* is another thin-shelled, freshwater gastropod. It lives in lakes, and can be found fossilized with *Planorbis* and other molluscs, along with plant and algal remains. Galba feeds on the algae adhering to plant surfaces. The fossil assemblage associated with *Galba* often indicates a subtropical climate.

CRUCIBULUM

Crucibulum is a type of limpet, commonly referred to as 'slipper limpets'. The shell is shaped like a low cone with an open base (see image on the opposite page). On the outer surface there are ribs that radiate from the apex and faint growth lines following the

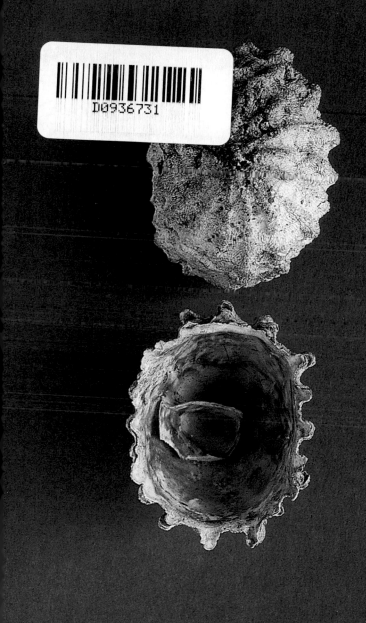

shell outline. The inside of the shell is smooth, and there is an internal structure on which the digestive organs are supported. The name 'cup and saucer shells' is used because of this secondary internal 'shell'.

Size: The genus grows to about 50mm (2in) in height.

Occurrence: Found in rocks of Miocene to Recent age in Europe, North America and the West Indies. The specimen is from Virginia, USA.

Comments: *Crucibulum* starts life as a male and after three or four years changes sex and becomes female. This is the usual life cycle for slipper limpets. The females are less active than the younger males, and stick to the seabed or to dead shells.

BIVALVES

ANTHRACONAUTA

This bivalve mollusc has a thin, delicate, equivalve shell. It is ovoid, with a slight posterior elongation away from the small, pointed umbo. The shell surface is ornamented with numerous concentric growth lines.

Size: This genus grew to around 50mm (2in) in length.

Occurrence: Found in strata of Carboniferous and Permian age in Europe.

Comments: *Anthraconauta* lived in fresh water, and is found fossilized in the non-marine strata deposited by rivers, streams and swamps that covered the Upper Carboniferous deltas. Bivalve molluscs are not usually suited for relative dating of rocks because they generally evolve slowly and individual species occur for longer

than is useful. However, in the Upper Carboniferous a zonal system has been established based on non-marine bivalves.

CARBONICOLA

Carbonicola has a relatively thick, equivalve shell, which is elongated posteriorly. There are strong, concentric growth lines but no

MOLLUSCS

other ornamentation. The hinge line is curved, and the beaks on each valve, which make up the umbo, bend slightly towards each other. On the inside of each valve, just below the beak, is a triangular pit, near which there may be two large hinge teeth.

Size: This genus grew to about 50mm (2in) in length.

Occurrence: Found in strata of Carboniferous age in Russia and Europe. The specimen illustrated is from West Yorkshire, UK.

Comments: *Carbonicola* is another non-marine bivalve mollusc associated with the stream deposits formed on Upper Carboniferous deltas. It probably burrowed into the stream-bed sediment, and pushed its shell into the mud with its fleshy foot. It is often compared with the genus *Unio*.

DUNBARELLA

This genus has a fan-like appearance, produced by its relatively flat valves crossed by numerous thin, radiating ribs. Concentric growth lines are also present. There is a long, straight hinge line, which, if complete, may have small winged extensions. The hinge teeth inside the valves, below the umbo, are insignificant.

Size: The genus is generally about 50mm (2in) along the hinge line.

Occurrence: *Dunbarella* is found in strata of Carboniferous age in North America and Europe.

Comments: Often this genus is fossilized in dark shales (as in the illustration above), crushed on the bedding planes. In this situation, accompanying fossils are those of goniatites (cephalopod molluscs) and other bivalves. Also, there are occasionally very small molluscan fossils including both bivalves and gastropods. These are probably juveniles. The dark shales are compacted mud, which formed in an

oxygen-poor seabed environment, and this may well account for the comparative lack of sea-floor organisms fossilized here.

HIPPOPODIUM

Hippopodium has a massive, thickened shell with an overall bi-convex shape. The two valves are equal in size. The shell surface is heavily textured and ornamented with numerous strong growth lines. There is a posterior extension to the shell.

Size: The genus grew to around 80mm (3⅛in) in length.

Occurrence: In rocks of Jurassic age in Europe and East Africa.

Comments: Some molluscan shells develop a thicker structure when they are mature, but *Hippopodium* secreted thickened shell material throughout its life, making the shell very heavy and awkward. It probably lived mainly buried in muddy or sandy sediment. It is found fossilized with ammonites, crinoids, other bivalves and belemnites.

SCHIZODUS

Schizodus is characterized by a thick shell with little ornamentation. There may be very faint growth lines on the smooth shell, which is slightly elongated posteriorly, a characteristic feature of a bivalve that burrowed into soft sediment. The shell edges are flattened, while the beak points inwards and upwards. On the inside of the valves there is a single large hinge tooth.

Size: This genus grew to around 50mm (2in) in width.
Occurrence: In strata of Carboniferous and Permian age, worldwide. The specimens illustrated are from Durham, UK.
Comments: Different species of the genus lived in a variety of environments. In Carboniferous strata, *Schizodus* occurs with other bivalve molluscs, nautiloids, brachiopods and crinoids in limestones formed on the slopes of marine reefs. Permian species of *Schizodus* are found with very few other organisms, including gastropods and bivalves, in marl (calcite-rich mudstone). This rock was formed in a high-salinity, landlocked basin where conditions were very harsh.

CARDINIA

This genus has an ovoid shell, which is extended in a posterior direction, and the umbo points anteriorly. The two sub-oval valves are similar. The ornamentation consists of thick, concentric growth lines. Larger shells are thicker, usually a feature of maturity in bi-valve molluscs.
Size: Large shells reach up to 200mm (8in) in width.
Occurrence: In rocks of Triassic and Jurassic age, worldwide.
Comments: *Cardinia* burrowed into soft, seabed sediment, with the

posterior end of the shell just level with the sediment surface. This bivalve probably fed on organic material suspended in the water. It is a common fossil in siltstones and clays of Jurassic age, where it occurs with fossils of ammonites, other bivalves (especially oysters), crinoids and burrowing arthropods.

OXYTOMA

An unusually shaped bivalve, *Oxytoma* has a spine-like extension protruding from one of the small 'wings' that lie beside the umbo. The shell has one flat valve and one convex valve, and the beak points upwards. Ornamentation consists of strong, widely spaced ribs ending as short spines, which reach beyond the shell margin.

Growth lines are also present.

Size: The genus grew to around 60mm (2⅖in) in length.

Occurrence: Found in rocks of Triassic, Jurassic and Cretaceous age, worldwide.

Comments: *Oxytoma* lived on the seabed or attached to floating material such as driftwood. As with many modern bivalves, such as the mussels, this genus used thread called byssus, made of brown coloured protein, to attach itself.

VENERICARDIA

This mollusc has very strong, similar valves, both being markedly convex. The beaks point forwards, and the shell is elongated in a posterior direction. Ornamentation on the outside of the valves consists of numerous wide, flat-topped ribs with narrow grooves between them. The margins of the valves have wavy crenulations. There are large hinge teeth on the inside of the valves.

Size: A large shell growing up to 150mm (6in) across.

Occurrence: In Palaeocene and Eocene strata in North America, Europe and Africa. The specimen illustrated is from Hampshire, UK.

Comments: *Venericardia* lived in a shallow burrow, with the posterior end uppermost. This, and the many other bivalve molluscs found fossilized with it, lived in shallow marine conditions on a seabed of sand and silt. A thick shell such as that of *Venericardia* would withstand turbulent conditions in shallow water.

PHOLADOMYA

This genus is equivalve, with a sub-oval, biconvex shell. Of particular note are the posterior elongation and the gape between the two valves at this end of the shell. The gape is a permanent opening, typical of burrowing bivalves, and through it the siphons extended up to the seabed surface, allowing the animal to draw water, containing suspended food, into the shell, and to expel waste. In this genus the siphons are never fully retracted. Because of the gape, fossil specimens are frequently infilled with sediment, and so are three-dimensionally preserved. The thin shell surface is ornamented with growth lines and fine granules. Inside there are no hinge teeth, but along the interior margin the pallial line has a deep sinus, another feature typical of a burrowing bivalve.

Size: *Pholadomya* grows to around 120mm (4⅝in) in length.

Occurrence: In strata of Triassic to Recent age, worldwide. The specimen illustrated is from Gloucestershire, UK.

Comments: Evidence from the rocks in which fossils of this mollusc shell are found suggests that in the past it lived in shallow marine conditions. Today it lives in deep, warm waters in the Atlantic Ocean and around the West Indies.

GRYPHAEA

This is one of the best known fossil bivalves and has been given a number of vernacular names, including 'devil's toenail'. The oyster has a shell unlike many bivalves because the two valves are dissimilar. There is one massive, curved valve and a smaller, thin valve resting inside the larger one. The larger shell is thickened by numerous growth increments, seen in the sectioned specimen illustrated. On the shell surface there are many growth lines, and the incurved umbo, commonly slightly twisted to one side, is characteristic. There are a number of species, some being much wider than the illustrated example.

Size: The illustrated species, *Gryphaea arcuata*, grew up to around 160mm (6⅜in) in length, but specimens are usually smaller.

Occurrence: Found in strata of Triassic and Jurassic age, worldwide. The examples shown are from North Yorkshire, UK.

Comments: This bivalve has a shell well suited to its sedentary lifestyle. When young, it was attached to the seabed by a byssus, but in adult life one valve became very thick and it rested on the seabed, with the massive valve on the sediment surface.

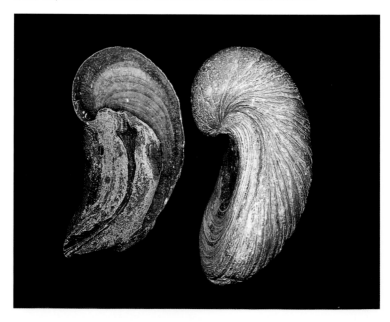

INOCERAMUS

This genus is inequivalve, and one of the valves is more convex than the other. The hinge line is straight, and there is a winged extension in some forms. There are no hinge teeth inside the shell. The exterior of the shell is ornamented with few thick ribs and many faint growth lines. Shells of this genus become much larger and thicker in the Upper Cretaceous period, before its extinction.

Size: It grew to around 120mm (4⅝in) in length.

Occurrence: Found in Jurassic and Cretaceous rocks, worldwide.

Comments: *Inoceramus* lived attached by its byssus to rocks or floating matter such as algae and driftwood. Fossils of this genus occur in Jurassic strata with ammonites, other bivalves and brachiopods, but it is probably best known from the chalk of Cretaceous age. In the past Inoceramus was used as a stratigraphic index fossil in this period, but that use has now been superseded. It occurs with fossils of echinoids, sponges, and other molluscs in Cretaceous strata.

MOLLUSCS

SPONDYLUS

Long spines, the main feature of this bivalve, are often broken off in fossils. In the illustrated example, only the stumps of the spines are visible. The shell is inequivalve, and one valve is more convex than the other. The outside of the shell is ornamented with growth lines and strong ribs. Internally, there is a single large muscle scar. The straight hinge line may have small, ear-like extensions, and the umbo points to one side.

Size: This genus grows to around 120mm (4⅝in) in length.

Occurrence: Found in rocks of Jurassic to Recent age, worldwide.

Comments: In life, *Spondylus* is anchored to the seabed. Modern forms live in tropical waters, and are attached when young. The spines help to spread the weight of the shell on soft sediment surfaces, and hold the shell above the seabed.

CEPHALOPODS

ISORTHOCERAS

This genus is a form of orthocone nautiloid, a group which developed throughout the Lower Palaeozoic and became extinct in the Triassic period. The shell is typically orthocone, being straight and tapering, with a circular cross-section. There are many chambers divided by septa, which are concave towards the shell aperture. The sutures, where the septa meet the shell wall, are simple. Through the centre of each septum is a hole marking the position of the siphuncle. A small, globular structure, the protoconch, is present at the narrow end of some shells. This was the original shell of the juvenile animal. The body chamber, at the wider end of the shell, is rarely preserved in fossils.

Size: Generally this genus grew to 100mm (4in) in length. Individuals of the related genus *Orthoceras* grew to several metres (yds) long.

Occurrence: In strata of Ordovician age, worldwide. The specimen illustrated is from the Maquokota formation in Iowa, USA.

Comments: *Isorthoceras* swam above the seabed, with the narrow end of the shell held uppermost by the buoyancy chambers. It is fossilized in a variety of different rocks because it was not reliant on seabed conditions. In some areas great masses of the shells are fossilized together, creating 'Orthoceras limestone', which is collected and polished for ornamental use.

MOLLUSCS

GONIATITES

This genus has a shell coiled in a flat spiral, with a sunken umbilicus on each side. This umbilicus is narrow, as the shell is involute, the outer whorl obscuring the inner ones. The sectioned specimen shows the coiling and also the septa dividing the shell into buoyancy chambers. The outside of the shell has spiral lines and delicate growth lines. Where the outermost surface of the shell is missing, suture lines may be seen. These have an almost zigzag shape, and are very simple compared with those of ammonites.

Size: *Goniatites* grew to around 50mm (2in) in diameter.
Occurrence: This genus is found in rocks of Carboniferous age in North America, North Africa, Asia and Europe.
Comments: As free-swimming ammonoids are used in the Mesozoic, *Goniatites* is used as a zone fossil in the Carboniferous. It is found in a variety of different rock types, and can be used to correlate these varying environments. *Goniatites*, the genus, is a member of the order Goniatitida (the goniatites), in which there are many genera.

CLYMENIA

This genus has a smooth, narrow shell, which is ornamented only with faint growth lines. The evolute shell is made of whorls that gradually increase in size from the tiny umbilicus to the large body chamber. Simple suture lines mark the position of the septa and, unusually for an ammonoid, the siphuncle is on the dorsal side of each whorl. (Other ammonoids have a ventral siphuncle.)
Size: *Clymenia* grew to around 80mm (3⅛in) in diameter.
Occurrence: From strata of Devonian age in Asia, Europe and North Africa.

Comments: Species of this genus are used as zone fossils in Upper Devonian rocks, along with goniatites. *Clymenia* became extinct at the end of Devonian time, unlike the goniatites, which continued into the Carboniferous. It was a free-swimming ammonoid, found in off-shore marine strata.

MONOPHYLLITES

Monophyllites has a narrow, disc-like shell with an oval cross-section. The coiling is involute, most of the whorls being obscured by the large outer whorl. There is very little ornamentation on the thin shell, apart from numerous faint growth lines, which curve

forwards as they approach the ventral surface of the shell.
Size: The genus reached about 100mm (4in) in diameter.
Occurrence: Found in strata of Triassic age in North America, Europe and Asia.
Comments: During the Triassic period, much of the present North Atlantic region was land, with hostile, hot, arid conditions. To the south of this area of land, shelf seas and deeper marine conditions existed, where molluscs like *Monophyllites* lived.

PSILOCERAS

The shell has sub-evolute coiling, each whorl being visible but over-lapping slightly. The whorls are rounded in cross-section. Commonly this ammonite is found crushed on the bedding planes of lower Jurassic shale, but here the shells are preserved in three dimensions. Fine, wavy ribs cross the shell, but in this example the shell is missing in many of the specimens. Suture lines are visible on the largest individual shown here. Some of these specimens must be virtually complete, as the sutureless body chambers can be seen.
Size: *Psiloceras* grew to a maximum diameter of about 70mm (2⅜in).

Occurrence: This genus occurs in the lowermost Jurassic rocks in Europe, Indonesia, North America and South America. The specimen is from North Yorkshire, UK.

Comments: *Psiloceras planorbis*, a species within the genus *Psiloceras*, is of considerable stratigraphic importance, as it is the zone index species for the lowest zone in the Jurassic system. Below its occurrence, rocks are of Triassic age.

ARNIOCERAS

On this specimen many individuals are preserved, some smooth, with the shell worn away, others more complete. Body chambers and suture lines are clearly seen on several examples. The shell has evolute coiling. Along the venter there is a sharp keel, which has a thin groove running along either side. Thick ribs radiate from the umbilicus and curve towards the shell aperture where they reach the ventral surface.

Size: This genus grew to about 50mm (2in) in diameter.

Occurrence: *Arnioceras* occurs in rocks of Lower Jurassic age,

MOLLUSCS

worldwide. The specimen is from Dorset, UK.

Comments: The species *Arnioceras semicostatum* is a zone fossil used in the Lower Jurassic.

DACTYLIOCERAS

The shell has evolute coiling, and is described as serpenticone (like a coiled snake). The ribs radiate from the umbilicus, and are closely spaced. Where the ribs cross the rounded ventral surface, they split into two. A number of species of this genus have been named. These differ in their coiling and in the ornamentation on the shell surface. Some have rows of tubercles; others have much finer ribbing. *Dactylioceras* is a very common genus, and in places occurs in great numbers.

Size: This genus grew to a maximum diameter of around 100mm (4in).

Occurrence: *Dactylioceras* occurs in rocks of Lower Jurassic age, worldwide. The illustrated specimens are from Holzmaden, Germany.

Comments: In North Yorkshire, UK, it was once believed that these fossils were the remains of snakes that had been turned to stone by St Hilda. She founded the Abbey at Whitby, on the top of the Jurassic cliffs in which the ammonite is so common. Local fossils often had snake-like heads carved on them (see p.15).

SPIROCERAS

Spiroceras as a genus has a very variable, uncoiled shell, in which the typical ammonite symmetry is lost, as it may coil in a slight 'corkscrew' spiral. The main ornamentation consists of thick ribs, orientated perpendicular to the shell axis. On the ventral surface there may be smooth areas, and in some species the venter has rows of tubercles.

Size: *Spiroceras* grew to around 75mm (3in) in diameter.
Occurrence: Found in strata of Jurassic age in Europe, Russia and Africa.
Comments: This genus is very like many ammonites found in Cretaceous strata, when uncoiling of the shell became quite common. It is thought that this type of ammonite shell was suited to a sessile, benthonic mode of life, and not to the more typical, free-swimming ammonite existence.

LIPAROCERAS (M) AND AEGOCERAS (m)

These two ammonite shells (see image on p.180) are believed to be the male and female, a dimorphic pair, of the same species (see p.182). They show very similar features, and the small *Aegoceras* is virtually the same as the inner whorls of *Liparoceras*. Studies of the evolution of these two ammonites show that they developed the same characteristics at the same time. Both have strong ribs that split across the venter, and similar sub-evolute coiling.

MOLLUSCS

Size: *Liparoceras* grew to around 100mm (4in) in diameter, and Aegoceras reached 60mm (2⅜in) in diameter.
Occurrence: In strata of Lower Jurassic age in Europe, North Africa and Indonesia. The specimens are from Gloucestershire, UK.
Comments: Because they were originally named before their sexual dimorphism was recognized, they have different scientific names.

ASTEROCERAS

The shell has widely spaced, thick ribs, and a keel, with a slight furrow on either side, runs along the venter (see image on the opposite page). The ribs do not cross the keel, and curve slightly towards the aperture as they reach the ventral surface. This specimen is ideal for illustrating some of the aspects of ammonite shell structure. The body chamber, reaching from the shell aperture for about half of a whorl, has been infilled with dark sediment. It has thus been preserved three-dimensionally, and has not been crushed by overlying sediment. The rest of the shell is pale in colour, and shows the complex suture lines. These mark the partitions between the buoyancy chambers, and so are not present on the body chamber.
Size: This genus grew to a maximum diameter of about 100mm (4in).
Occurrence: *Asteroceras* occurs in rocks of Lower Jurassic age. It is found in Europe, Asia and North America.
Comments: The species *Asteroceras obtusum* is a zone fossil in the Lower Jurassic.

SEXUAL DIMORPHISM IN AMMONITES

Research has shown that some ammonites, previously thought to be different species, developed the same characteristics at the same time during their evolution, and became extinct at the same time. It is now generally believed that they are males and females of the same species. These ammonite shells usually fall into two distinct size categories, a small microconch (m) and a larger macroconch (M). Modern cephalopods show this size difference between the sexes: for example, the female Paper Nautilus, *Argonauta argo*, is 20 times larger than the male! With fossils, it is difficult to say if the macroconch is male or female, though many palaeontologists regard the larger shell as the female. In order for the size comparison to be made, only complete, mature shells can be studied.

PROMICROCERAS

This genus is characterized by an evolute shell, with the individual whorls overlapping only slightly; all the whorls are clearly visible. In cross-section the whorls are rounded. Thick, well-spaced ribs cross the shell and radiate from the central umbilicus. As the ribs reach the ventral surface they curve slightly and become flattened.

Size: The individuals in this genus grew to a maximum diameter of 30mm (1⅛in).

Occurrence: This ammonite is found in rocks of Lower Jurassic age, and is restricted geographically to Europe.

Comments: The specimen illustrated shows a mass of shells packed tightly together and making up virtually the whole of the rock. It is from the famous Marston 'marble' found in Somerset, UK. Ammonites are not often fossilized in such great numbers together. Some of the ammonites here have their original pale-coloured shell still in place, while in certain individuals this has been broken off to reveal the complex suture lines. Where shells are cut in half, the individual internal buoyancy chambers are visible.

KOSMOCERAS

Kosmoceras is ornamented with tubercles, spines and ribs that bifurcate (split in two) across the venter. The specimen illustrated shows this ornamentation, and it also has a lappet extending from the aperture. As is typical with shells found in clay and shale, this specimen has been crushed.

Size: The genus grew to a diameter of about 60mm (2⅜in).

Occurrence: In rocks of Middle Jurassic age, worldwide.

Comments: Detailed studies of species within this genus suggest that they show sexual dimorphism. Within certain strata the fossils exhibit differences, including the size of the shell and its ornamentation. This may mean that one size group are males, and the other, females.

PERISPHINCTES

This genus has an evolute shell, with all the whorls clearly visible. The ornamentation consists of closely packed ribs, which are stouter on the final whorl. If the shell is complete and the body chamber is present, this area of the shell near the aperture can be smooth. The ribs split into two or three where they cross the venter. The whorls have an almost square cross-section.

Size: A large ammonite, specimens of *Perisphinctes* are often over 200mm (8in) in diameter.

Occurrence: Found in Jurassic strata in Europe, Africa, Japan, Pakistan and Cuba. The illustrated specimen is from Madagascar.

Comments: Sexual dimorphism has been recognized in this ammonite, on the usual grounds of size. Both the macroconch (the large shelled form) and the microconch have virtually identical features, with the exception that the microconch has a lappet on the shell aperture. This extension of the shell (see *Kosmoceras*, p.183) is found on many microconch forms.

PAVLOVIA

Pavlovia has a shell with evolute coiling, the inner whorls and umbilicus being clearly visible. Strong, sharply edged ribs, which bifurcate as they cross the venter, ornament the shell. The ribs are more closely

packed on the inner whorls. The pale material on the illustrated specimen is probably the remains of the animal's original shell.

Size: This large ammonite reached about 400mm (16in) in diameter.

Occurrence: Found in rocks of Upper Jurassic age in Europe, Asia and Greenland.

Comments: Two species of this genus, *Pavlovia rotunda* and *Pavlovia pallasinoides*, are used as zone fossils. The specimen shown has had its shell infilled with dark-coloured mud, and this has preserved at least the outer whorl in three dimensions. Often the inner whorls of ammonites are crushed, because sediment cannot get into them past the septa.

TITANITES

With an evolute shell, *Titanites* is similar in general shape to many ammonite genera. The ornamentation consists of ribs that birfurcate across the venter and crowd together near the shell aperture, where they curve forwards. The crowding of the ribs is a feature

that helps to prove if a shell is complete. Ammonite shell growth seems to have slowed as the animal reached maturity.

Size: This is one of the largest ammonites, frequently reaching over 1m (39in) in diameter.

Occurrence: In strata of Upper Jurassic age in Europe, Asia, Canada and Greenland. The specimen illustrated is from Dorset, UK.

Comments: Two species of *Titanites* are used as zone fossils for rocks in the Jurassic period.

DOUVILLEICERAS

This ammonite has a sub-evolute shell, with the whorls overlapping about half their height. The ornamentation consists of very prominent ribs, which do not split as they cross the venter, where they develop large nodes, giving the shell a knobbly appearance. In some shells the outermost whorl lacks these tubercles.

Size: The genus is typically around 50mm (2in) in diameter.

Occurrence: In strata of Cretaceous age in North America, South America, Europe, India and Madagascar. The specimen shown is from France.

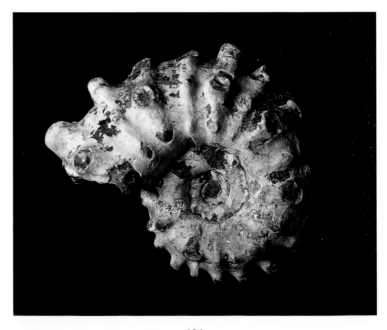

Comments: A species of this genus, *Douvilleiceras mammillatum* is a zone fossil in the Cretaceous period. The specimen shows original shell material and an infilling of brownish sediment, some of which also adheres to the outside of the shell.

BACULITES

A whole specimen of this ammonite has one or two small, coiled whorls, with a long, straight shell gradually widening from them. More frequently, broken sections, as shown here, are found. The straight part of the shell is compressed, with an oval cross-section. Ornamentation is often lacking, but in some species the shell is ribbed, with tubercles on the venter. The aperture has a long extension, called a rostrum, developed from its dorsal margin.

Size: Commonly, fossils of this genus are a few centimetres in length, but *Baculites* could grow to 2m (78in) long.

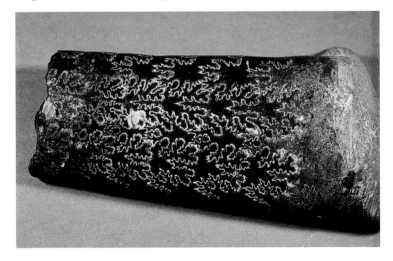

Occurrence: Found in strata of Cretaceous age, worldwide. The specimen illustrated is from South Dakota, USA.

Comments: In the early part of the Cretaceous period, *Baculites* only grew to a small size. The largest shells are from the late Cretaceous period.

SCAPHITES

This ammonite genus is unusual in that the shell is partly uncoiled. The inner whorls are involute and coiled tightly, while the outer whorl, containing the body chamber, is uncoiled and ends in a hook. This part of the shell is often missing in fossils. Overall, the shell is wide and flat, with a constricted aperture. Shell ornamentation consists of closely spaced ribs, which curve forwards as they cross the venter, and rows of tubercles.

Size: *Scaphites* grew to about 75mm (3in) in width.

Occurrence: In strata of Cretaceous age in North America, Chile, southern Africa, Madagascar and Australia.

Comments: There has been much discussion as to the orientation of this unusual shell during the animal's life. It is likely that it lived

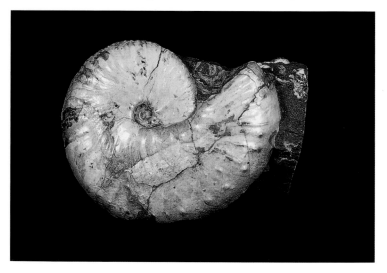

with the uncoiled body chamber underneath, and the aperture facing upwards. *Scaphites* was probably not an active swimmer, finding lateral movement difficult.

CENOCERAS

This is the shell of a nautiloid, and though outwardly similar to the ammonoids, there are many important differences. The coiling of *Cenoceras*, like that of the modern *Nautilus pompilius*, is involute,

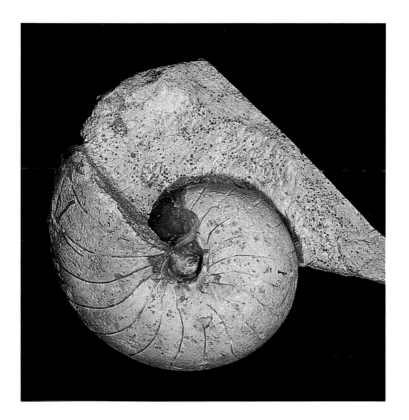

the last whorl completely obscuring the inner whorls. In this specimen the outer shell has worn off, and the simple suture lines can be seen. These are very different from the complex ammonoid sutures. The outer shell, when present, is smooth, with very faint growth lines. The siphuncle in nautiloids runs through the centre of each septum, not along the ventral surface as in ammonoids.

Size: The genus grew to around 150mm (6in) in diameter.

Occurrence: *Cenoceras* is found in strata of Triassic and Jurassic age, worldwide.

Comments: The modern *Nautilus* lives in warm, tropical seas around South-East Asia and Australia. However, dead shells are carried across the Indian Ocean and north to Japan. This suggests that dead ammonite shells, which had a similar system of buoyancy chambers, could also drift some distance.

ACROCOELITES

These cylindrical, pointed fossils are belemnites, part of the internal solid structure of a squid-like mollusc. Belemnites are usually smooth, and at the wider end may have the remains of a structure called the phragmacone. This is divided into chambers, and has a central siphuncle. The fossils seen here are referred to as guards. They are made of calcite, and this is built up in layers, which can be seen in some of the broken specimens shown here. Around the guards and phragmacone was the animal's soft body, with its head bearing, at the wider end, tentacles, a funnel and eyes.

Size: This genus grew to around 100mm (4in) in length.

Occurrence: Found in strata of Jurassic age in North America and Europe.

Comments: The belemnite's funnel was used, as in other cephalopods, for jet propulsion. Belemnite fossils have been found with ink sacs so, like some modern cephalopods, belemnites were able to emit a cloud of ink for concealment.

VERTEBRATE FOSSILS

Fossils of vertebrate creatures are far less common that those of invertebrates such as molluscs, arthropods and echinoderms. Vertebrates evolved much later, so their occurrence as fossils is more limited stratigraphically. Also, many vertebrates live on land, where weathering and erosion remove rock and loose sediment. A skeleton on land, even if it is covered by sand or mud, may soon be broken and destroyed by erosion. There are nevertheless some parts of the world where huge numbers of vertebrate fossils have been discovered. China, Africa and North America are sources of many dinosaur and other skeletons. Often the localities in these areas are remote and difficult to reach. Fossils of fish and marine reptiles are not uncommon. They are fossilized in rocks formed on the seabed, where disturbance is far less, and preserved just as easily as molluscs and other invertebrates. The remains of these creatures are usually fragmented, and a single tooth may be all that is left. Vertebrate skeletons are held in a fleshy body, and when this decays, or is scavenged, the bones soon become disarticulated. Bone itself is reasonably durable, while teeth and some fish scales are also very resistant, both chemically and physically, so they are easily fossilized. The vertebrate fossils illustrated in this chapter have been chosen because they are the type of material most often encountered.

Fossil Fish Evolution

The earliest group of fish to be found as fossils are classified as agnathans. In Wyoming, USA, small pieces of bone from these fish are the earliest vertebrate remains in rocks of Cambrian age. Agnathans are a group without jaws, and many had thin, heavily armoured bodies. The ostracoderms are the main fossil representatives within the agnathan class, which today contains the scale-less, eel-like lampreys. During the late Silurian and Devonian periods, fish evolved rapidly. with a number of groups developing. The placo-derms, which are now extinct, had primitive jaws and paired fins. These fish were the most common vertebrates towards

OPPOSITE: Great numbers of fossil fish, like the specimens shown here, died when river or lake systems dried up. This example is from Cenozoic strata, and was found in China.

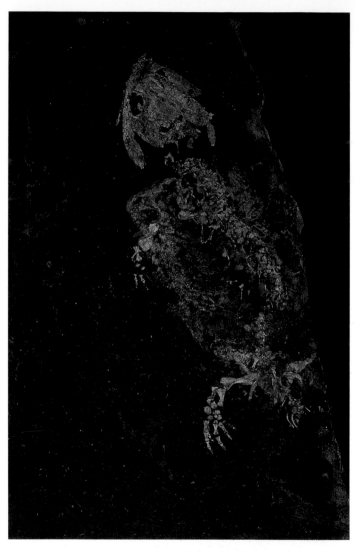

ABOVE: This amphibian belongs to a group called temnospondyls. The specimen is from Carboniferous strata in southern Scotland, UK. Similar fossils are known from West Virginia, USA; Nova Scotia, Canada; Greenland and Australia.

the end of the Devonian period. Other jawed fish include the Chondrichthyes. Some fish within this group have skeletons made of cartilage, and sharks such as *Carcharodon* are classified here. The final important group are the Osteichthyes. These are the bony fish, common and widespread today, which first appear as fossils in the Devonian period. Within this group the teleosts are the most numerous, and the crossopterygians have many similarities with amphibians.

Amphibians and Reptiles

During the Devonian period, amphibians seem to have evolved from the fish. Fossils of the earliest amphibians have been discovered in Greenland. The forest swamps that flourished during the Late Carboniferous were an ideal habitat for amphibians. Creatures such as temnospondyls lived at this time and depended on the swamp lakes and streams for egg-laying and development of their young. Fossils of amphibians similar to those living today – newts, salamanders and frogs – first occur in Triassic strata.

Alongside the early amphibians, reptiles evolved during the Carboniferous period. A great step forward for the reptiles was the ability to reproduce without water. Their amniote eggs had tough shells, and there was no need for a larval stage as the young developed entirely within the eggs. The best known reptiles are the dinosaurs. The giant sauropodomorphs, such as *Brachiosaurus* and *Diplodocus*, which fed on vegetation, may have weighed over 30 tonnes. A second major group was the theropods. *Tyrannosaurus* belonged to this group, as did other large carnivores. It has recently been suggested that *Tyrannosaurus* was not a fierce predator, as originally thought, but probably a scavenger. The third group of dinosaurs, the ornithischians, was a varied group including large and small dinosaurs, some bipeds, others quadrupeds. *Iguanodon* was one of the larger ornithiscians at around 10m (33ft) long, and many in this group developed heavily armoured bodies and head shields like those on *Triceratops*. As well as dinosaurs, other reptiles are well known as fossils. These include crocodiles, the marine ichthyosaurs and plesiosaurs, and flying pterosaurs.

Dinosaur Extinction

The reason for the extinction of the dinosaurs at the end of the Cretaceous period has been the subject of much debate. Their

ABOVE: Bone bed with vertebrate remains. Vertebrate bones, teeth and other remains are often fossilized as fragments washed together by rivers or sea currents. This specimen of Triassic age contains numerous bone fragments and fish scales.

demise was not as sudden as is often thought, and may have taken a million years. Along with the dinosaurs, many marine organisms died out at this time, including 75 percent of marine plankton and successful groups such as the ammonites. However, mammals, birds and cephalopods such as squids and *Nautilus* survived.

Two factors may have contributed to dinosaur extinction: climate change and meteorite impact. Evidence shows that the sea level fell at the end of the Cretaceous period. This would have caused a rise in worldwide temperatures because of the smaller area covered by the moderating oceans.

A study of oxygen isotopes in Cretaceous limestones proves this temperature rise. It is generally accepted that a large meteorite hit the Earth in late Cretaceous times. The presence of iridium in clay, and shocked quartz around where the impact may have occurred, are evidence of this. Dust and rock fragments from the impact would have filled the sky and obscured the sunlight. Plants would have died out, and food chains would have been destroyed.

There are many instances of exciting dinosaur and other vertebrate finds being made by amateur palaeontologists; indeed, the bones of one of the first large dinosaurs to be unearthed, *Iguanodon*, were found by a doctor's wife in Sussex, UK. More recently, a number of dinosaur skeletons have been discovered by amateur fossil hunters working on the Isle of Wight, UK, including what may be the largest sauropod in Europe.

The Evolution of Mammals

The fossils of small, shrew-like mammals have been found in strata of Jurassic and Cretaceous age. The Cretaceous rocks of Mongolia are a source of many of these fossils. Mammals were able to evolve rapidly and take over new habitats during the Cenozoic era, after the demise of the dinosaurs. Herbivorous Cenozoic mammals often grew to great size. *Indricotherium* resembled a giant rhinoceros and measured over 5m (16ft) at its shoulder. This and many other genera took advantage of the spread of grassland habitats, and were preyed on by carnivores such as tigers. Mammals diversified and took to the air. *Icaronycteris* is an early fossil bat, and *Colugo* a fossilized gliding lemur. Matching the size of some of the giant herbivorous mammals, *Basilosaurus*, a vast whale found fossilized in rocks of Miocene age, grew to 25m (80ft) in length. Many of the Cenozoic mammals became extinct around 20,000 years ago, but no definite cause is known.

CEPHALASPIS

This small fish has a well-armoured body with a large head shield. There are curved extensions, reminiscent of a trilobite's genal spines. *Cephalaspis* has sensory areas on the head, which may have been able to detect changes in water pressure, and two small eyes high up, close together, in the middle. The thin, elongated body is not unlike that of a modern eel or lamprey, and gradually tapers to a thin point rather than a typical fish tail. The gills and mouth are on the underside of the head shield. *Cephalaspis* belongs to a group called the ostracoderms, which includes the oldest known vertebrates.
Size: The genus grew to around 100mm (4in) in length.
Occurrence: In strata of Silurian and Devonian age, worldwide.
Comments: *Cephalaspis* lived in the freshwater lakes on the great continent that covered what is now North America, Greenland and

north-western Europe. Other fossils found with *Cephalaspis* include further fish remains, plants and eurypterids. Research into the brain structure of these fishes suggests that they are similar to modern lampreys, primitive parasitic fishes.

HOLOPTYCHIUS

This fossil fish (see image on the opposite page) has more typically modern, fish-like characteristics than *Cephalaspis*. It is covered in large, rounded scales, that overlap like roof tiles. The lobed fins have bones within them, and the forked tail has bones in its lower part.
Size: The genus grew to around 500mm (20in) in length.

Occurrence: It is found in strata of Devonian and Carboniferous age, worldwide.

Comments: *Holoptychius* lived in freshwater lakes and rivers. In some exceptional circumstances, fossil fishes occur in great numbers. The famous deposits in Fife, Scotland, UK, from where the specimens illustrated come, have many fossils in one locality. These deposits, when mapped and studied in three dimensions, are seen to be small basins filled with sandstone, packed with fossil fishes. It is believed that during a period of drought, when rivers dried up, the fishes were trapped in pools, which in turn evaporated.

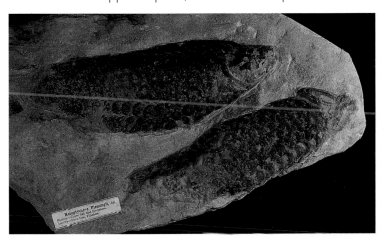

BOTHRIOLEPIS

This fossil fish is usually preserved, as here (see the image on the following page), only as a head shield. This is characterized by two long, fin-like structures, which could move independently. The head is armoured with a number of large, bony plates. These are rough, and covered in small nodes, giving a surface like coarse sandpaper. The slender tail section has no scales, and forks, with a large upper lobe.

Size: The whole fish grew to around 200mm (8in) in length.

Occurrence: In rocks of Devonian age, worldwide. The specimen is from the famous locality at Scaumenac Bay, Canada.

Comments: *Bothriolepis* is a placoderm fish, and has the simple jaws ad paired fins typical of the group.

CHEIROLEPIS

This genus has a relatively slender, scaly body, with small scales, almost square in shape. The fins are of interest, because they are supported by rays, as in many modern fishes. The tail has unequal lobes, the upper one being the larger, and there is a single dorsal fin.

Size: The genus grew to about 350mm (14in) in length.

Occurrence: In strata of Devonian age, worldwide.

Comments: *Cheirolepis* is an ancestor of the teleosts, which are the

dominant fishes today. It lived in freshwater lakes and rivers, and occurs with other fish, plant and arthropod remains, usually in fine-grained sandstone.

GYROPTICHIUS

Fish scales and teeth are made of durable material and are often found fossilized. This specimen, from Orkney, Scotland, UK, has a covering of dark, rhombic scales. The head is armoured with larger scales and plates. The slender body tapers gradually towards the tail, which is short and simple. Near the tail are two pairs of short, rounded fins.

Size: *Gyroptichius* grew to about 70mm (2⅖in) in length.
Occurrence: In strata of Devonian age, worldwide.
Comments: This fish is found in rocks formed in freshwater environments, often with other fishes such as *Cheirolepis* and *Dipterus*. It probably moved with an eel-like motion, and swam poorly near the bed of a lake or river.

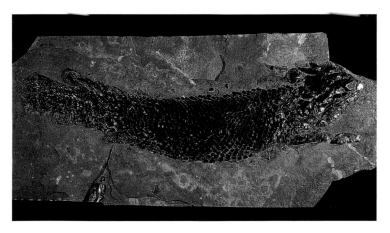

DIPTERUS

Dipterus has a short, stumpy body, with a relatively large head and tail (see image on p.202). The fins are strengthened with bony material. The tail has a large upper lobe. It was a jawed fish with flattened teeth that were probably used for crushing prey such as small, shelled invertebrates.

Size: This fish grew to about 70mm (2⅖in) in length.

Occurrence: In strata of Devonian age, worldwide. The specimen is from Achnaharras, Scotland, UK.

Comments: *Dipterus* is an important fossil because it has many of the features of modern lungfishes. It was probably able to survive

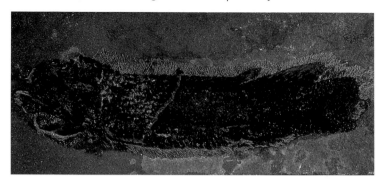

drought conditions (unlike other fishes, which died in large numbers as lake and river systems dried up) by obtaining oxygen from the atmosphere. The strengthened fins are vital, because they may have enabled *Dipterus* to move about in mud when the water dried up.

PLATYSOMUS

The wide body of this bony fish is covered with elongated scales in rows running from the dorsal to ventral surface. The head is covered in larger scales and plates, and the tail is symmetrical. There

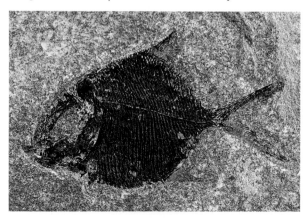

are large, triangular fins, and it is thought that *Platysomus* was an agile swimmer. The mouth contains cone-shaped teeth, designed for crushing prey.

Size: This genus grew to about 100mm (4in) in length.

Occurrence: *Platysomus* is found in rocks of Carboniferous and Permian age, worldwide.

Comments: This is a marine fish which has many modern characteristics, the single dorsal fin being typical. It is often fossilized with other fishes, the brachiopod *Lingula*, and plant remains.

CERATODUS

This fossil is the tooth of a lungfish called *Ceratodus*. With a rough, pitted surface, this fused structure could crush both plant and animal matter. Teeth are made of very resistant material, and often occur as the only fossil remains of an animal.

Size: The tooth illustrated is 20mm (⅘in) long.

Occurrence: Found in rocks of Triassic age, worldwide. The specimen is from a condensed deposit, known as a 'bone bed', that represents a considerable time span. Such deposits contain a high proportion of fossils, which are often of teeth and bone fragments. They usually formed when little sediment was being deposited.

Comments: The modern lungfish *Neoceratodus* lives today in Australia, and is probably similar to the fossil genus described here. Lungfishes have no bony skeleton; instead their body is supported with cartilage. They evolved during the Devonian period from fishes such as *Dipterus* (see pp.201–202). Using gills when underwater, and an air bladder when above water, lungfishes can survive buried in mud for some time.

CARCHARODON

This tooth, from the fossil shark *Carcharodon*, has a triangular outline, and is flattened, with sharp, serrated edges. Some shark teeth have side cusps, but *Carcharodon* lacks these. Skeletons from this genus are unusual in the fossil record – usually only the teeth are found.

Size: The tooth is typical at 50mm (2in) long, but they have been found 150mm (6in) in length.

Occurrence: The genus occurs in strata of Cenozoic to Recent age, worldwide.

Comments: The modern Great White Shark, *Carcharodon carcharias*, may grow to 9m (30ft) in length. This is a fierce predator with many human victims. The tooth shown here is from a species that may have reached 15m (50ft) in length.

DAPEDIUS

Typically this fish has a flattened, rounded shape and a covering of thick, bony plates, which take on the appearance and function of scales. These plates are rectangular in shape, and the fins and tail are supported by elongated, bony structures. The dorsal fin runs

from midway along the back to the tail; the anal fin is roughly half this length. There are numerous small teeth in the mouth.

Size: The genus grew to around 200mm (8in) in length.

Occurrence: Found in Jurassic strata, worldwide. The specimen is from Dorset, UK.

Comments: A marine fish which is found fossilized with ammonites, bivalve molluscs and crinoids. During the Jurassic period, fishes of this type, with bony outer coverings, were replaced by teleosts with modern features such as scales.

COCODUS

This slender fish has an elongate, ovoid body. The head is relatively large, ending in a sharp point, and has a long gape. The strong

205

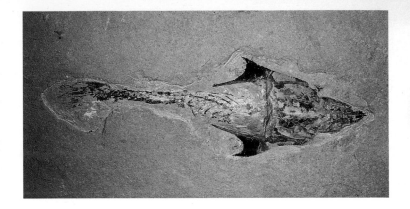

teeth are flattened and hemispherical. The fish has a number of spines: two thorn-shaped spines curving back from the head shield and a prominent dorsal spine.

Size: The genus grew to around 50mm (2in) in length.

Occurrence: In rocks of Cretaceous age in Europe and Asia. The specimen is from Lebanon.

Comments: Many fish fossils are found today in regions away from the sea that have arid climates. *Cocodus* and other fishes from the Middle East, along with the famous Green River deposits of Wyoming, USA, help palaeontologists to reconstruct past environments.

GOSUITICHTHYS

This freshwater genus is very like many modern fishes, belonging to the teleost group. The backbone is closer to the dorsal surface, and numerous slender ribs support the body (see image on the opposite page). The head is protected by scales larger than those on the body, and the tail is divided into two equal lobes.

Size: The genus grew to a maximum length of about 500mm (20in), though many specimens are much shorter than this.

Occurrence: Found in Cenozoic strata in North America. The example is from the Green River formation in Wyoming, USA.

Comments: Though this genus is found only in rocks in North America, it is a very well-known fossil. As with a number of different organisms that occur fossilized in great numbers, many specimens are offered for sale in various parts of the world.

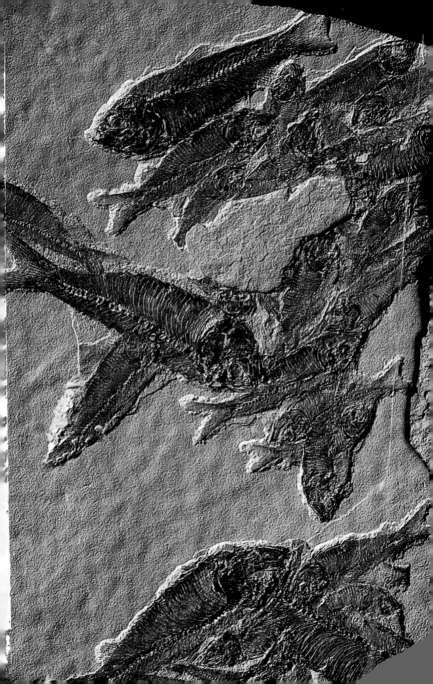

THE GREEN RIVER FORMATION

In some parts of the fossil record there are exceptional instances of preservation. The Green River formation in the eastern Rockies is one such example. There were, during the Eocene epoch, three distinct lake basins in the area of south-western Wyoming, mid-eastern Utah and mid-western Colorado. In these lakes lived many fishes, including *Gosuitichthys*, *Priscacara*, *Diplomystus* and *Knightia*. Fossils of these fishes are found in vast numbers, preserved on the bedding planes of fine-grained limestones. It seems that the fishes died in great numbers when at least part of the lake dried out from time to time. Research has shown that the lakes developed over about seven and a half million years, and that for much of the time there were distinct wet and dry seasons. Pollen found in the lake sediments suggests that luxuriant vegetation grew nearby, in a warm, moist climate.

KNIGHTIA

A teleost fish with many features similar to *Gosuitichthys*, *Knightia* has a vertebral column quite near the dorsal surface. The delicate ribs curve towards the tail, below the backbone. Its head has large protective plates and the tail is deeply forked, with equally sized lobes. The fins consist of pectoral, nearest the head, pelvic and anal, below the body, and a triangular dorsal fin midway along the back.

Size: This genus grew to 250mm (10in) in length.
Occurrence: Found in Eocene strata in North America. The example is from the Green River formation of Wyoming, USA.
Comments: Often fossils of the Green River fishes, such as *Knightia*, are found in a fragmented state. This may be a result of an internal eruption of gas, produced by decomposition.

LAMNA

This tooth is from a common shark genus called *Lamna*, whose mouth contained up to four rows of teeth. These are smooth, sometimes with vertical grooves, and are characterized by the two pointed extensions at the base.
Size: This tooth is 50mm (2in) long, and comes from a medium-

sized shark, nowhere near as gigantic as *Carcharodon* (see p.204).
Occurrence: Found in rocks of Cretaceous to Recent age, worldwide. The example shown is from Morocco.
Comments: Today, species of *Lamna*, a genus that includes the porbeagles, reach over 4m (13ft) in length, and tend to live in the temperate oceans. They eat squids and various fishes, and swim about in small shoals. It is probable that the fossil species had a similar lifestyle.

LEPTOLEPIS

This genus is a teleost, and has a long, tapering body with a central dorsal fin. As with many other teleosts, the backbone is near the dorsal surface and the tail has equal-sized lobes. There is a

the dorsal surface and the tail has equal-sized lobes. There is a relatively large head, and a wide eye socket is visible.

Size: A small fish, which grew to around 100mm (4in) in length.

Occurrence: Found in strata of Triassic to Cretaceous age in North America, Asia, South Africa and Europe. The specimen shown is from Germany.

Comments: This fish is common in the famous Solnhofen deposits of Germany. Here there are exceptional fossils, and *Leptolepis* often occurs in great numbers. The lagoon in which the fossil-bearing rocks were formed was a very hostile environment, and many of the fossils, possibly including *Leptolepis*, were washed in by storms.

MOSASAURUS

A tooth and part of the spinal column with ribs of this marine lizard are illustrated on the opposite page. The creature had a slender body, with a strong tail used for swimming. There were paddle-like limbs, but these are thought to have been for steering rather than providing power. The skull is very like that of a modern monitor lizard, even as far as small details like a joint in the jaw. The head was long, and the jaws armed with strong, pointed teeth, as seen here.

Size: The whole creature grew to 5–10m (16–33ft) in length. The tooth shown on the top of the opposite page is 50mm (2in) long.

Occurrence: In rocks of Cretaceous age from North America (many specimens are known from Kansas), and Northern Europe.

Comments: This large sea lizard was probably capable of catching fishes and other vertebrates. One species of *Mosasaurus* had

flattened teeth adapted for crushing, and may have eaten shellfish. There is an interesting history to the discovery and naming of this genus. As long ago as 1770, huge fossil jaws discovered in a chalk quarry near Maastricht in the Netherlands were of a then unknown creature. Some years later they were brought to the attention of George Cuvier. (He was to become famous for applying the principles of comparative anatomy to fossil material.) By comparing the fossil with living creatures, he recognized the jaws as belonging to a marine lizard, and it was named *Mosasaur*, as it was a reptile from the Meuse. This giant fossil also supported his theories about extinctions.

VERTEBRATE FOSSILS

PLESIOSAURUS

Plesiosaurus is another genus of marine reptile, whose fossilized bones are not uncommon. The body was broad, and had the support of a sturdy ribcage, a part of which is illustrated. The thick

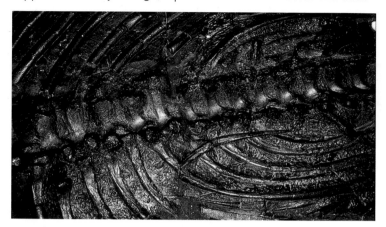

ribs and spinal column have been preserved here in dark shale. The head was relatively small, and was at the end of a long neck, which may well have been used to sling the head, armed with a mouth full of sharp teeth, at fish and other prey. The large, paddle-like limbs were for propulsion. A study of the musculature has shown that the paddles moved up and down in a similar manner to the wings of sea birds that swim underwater. The tail is short and stumpy.
Size: This genus grew up to 12m (39ft) in length.
Occurrence: In strata of Jurassic and Cretaceous age, worldwide. Some of the finest specimens are from North America and Europe.
Comments: The first *Plesiosaurus* to be discovered came from an area that is still a classic locality for these marine reptiles – Lyme Regis, Dorset, UK. It was found by Mary Anning in the early years of the 19th century. She became famous for the great variety of fossils she collected.

PLIOSAURUS

A close relative of the plesiosaurs, pliosaurs differed from them in a number of important ways, and evolved from them. The main difference was the length of the neck, with *Pliosaurus* having a very

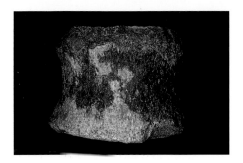

short neck and a large head. The massive teeth were blunt, more useful for grinding than cutting flesh apart. The illustration shows a vertebra that has been preserved in such a way as to show the bone structure in detail.

Size: This genus grew to over 10m (33ft) in length. The skull of one pliosaur from Australia is over 2.4m (8ft) long.

Occurrence: In rocks of Jurassic age, worldwide.

Comments: With a powerful body and tail, pliosaurs may have spent much time hunting for swimming creatures such as ammonites and fishes, and they may have lived at considerable depth. Pliosaurs, though reptiles, have often been likened to today's killer whales in their lifestyle and hunting habits.

ICHTHYOSAURUS

The material illustrated is a jaw fragment and some disarticulated bones. The teeth have a cone-shaped structure, with grooves running towards their sharp point. Among the typical assortment of bones are ribs and vertebrae. Ichthyosaurs had a streamlined body, with a large, vertically held tail, the lower lobe of which, supported

by vertebrae, was about twice the size of the upper one. There was a large dorsal fin and two pairs of paddle-like flippers on the ventral surface. The jaw was beak-like, and the large eyes were surrounded by a ring of small bones, possibly for protection.

Size: These creatures grew to around 3m (10ft) in length.

Occurrence: Found in rocks of Triassic, Jurassic and Cretaceous age, worldwide.

Comments: If the pliosaurs were similar in many respects to modern killer whales, the ichthyosaurs can be compared to porpoises and dolphins. They were fast swimmers, and fed on fish and cephalopod molluscs. In the stomach cavity of one ichthyosaur, the tentacle hooks of over 1,500 cephalopods have been found. Ichthyosaurs are frequently discovered fossilized in shales and other marine rocks, with ammonites and belemnites.

STEREOSTERNUM

This is the skeleton of a small reptile. The body and tail are elongated, while the head is slender and triangular, with many small, sharp teeth. The hind limbs have larger feet than the front pair. The feet were adapted like small paddles for swimming. *Stereosternum* probably ate fish.

Size: The genus grew to around 1m (39in) in length.

Occurrence: Found in strata of Triassic age in South America and southern Africa.

Comments: This reptile is classified as a mesosaur. These have a long palaeontological history, first being discovered in 1864 in southern Africa. In 1886, similar skeletons were discovered in Brazil. Today these continents are far apart, but there is much evidence to prove that, before the Cretaceous period, they were joined as part of the huge continent called Gondwanaland. In this landmass, Brazil and southern Africa were close together, and the finding of *Ste-*

reosternum in these two regions is an important piece of evidence for continental drift.

IGUANODON

This thick-set dinosaur was probably rather ungainly. The heavy body was supported by two large hind limbs, which had three-toed feet and hoof-like claws. The massive tail and neck helped to balance the creature as it moved. It probably had an upright posture, but may have moved on all fours at times. The front limbs

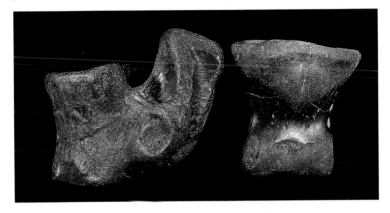

were adapted for clasping and tearing vegetation, having four fingers and a thumb spike. (In early reconstructions, this 'spike' caused problems, and was even placed on the animal's nose.) The snout was long, toothless and horny, and inside the mouth were teeth designed for grinding vegetation. The illustration shows a curving caudal vertebra and a toe bone.

Size: *Iguanodon* was around 10m (33ft) tall.

Occurrence: In Cretaceous strata in Europe, North America and North Africa.

Comments: This is one of the first dinosaurs to be described, and its discovery is an interesting story. It was named in 1825 by Gideon Mantell, a medical doctor who was a life-long amateur palaeontologist. In 1818, while Mantell was visiting a patient near Cuckfield in Sussex, UK, his wife found some fossil teeth in a tip of road-mending rubble. He recognized them to be from a large herbivore, but knew that no mammals had been found in the local Cretaceous rocks, and plant-eating reptiles were unknown to him. Colleagues suggested they were from a modern mammal, and when he sent the teeth to the great French palaeontologist, Baron Cuvier, he was told they were from a rhinoceros. Mantell had traced the roadstone to a particular quarry, and here he found bones from the creature, including the famous 'spike'. He was sure he had found something unusual, and that Cuvier was incorrect. He visited the Museum of the Royal College of Surgeons, where teeth he had found were matched very closely with those of a modern iguana. Mantell called his dinosaur *Iguanodon* after these reptiles. In 1834 Mantell acquired a skeleton of *Iguanodon* that had been found in a quarry at Maidstone in Kent, UK. In all, Mantell wrote over 60 books and articles, and in 1833 he found the remains of the first described armoured dinosaur, *Hylaeosaurus*.

CROCODILE

Large vertebrates such as crocodiles often become fragmented before fossilization. The dark, rough-surfaced fossil on the opposite page is a scute, or bony plate, from the tough armour of a crocodile's

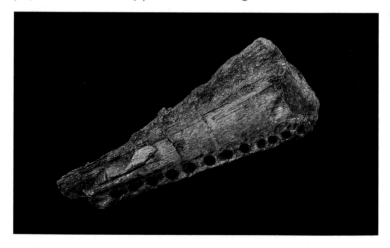

back. The elongated, pale-coloured fossil above is part of a crocodile's jaw, in which tooth sockets are clearly seen. Jurassic crocodiles had long, slender snouts, filled with sharp teeth for eating fishes and other prey. The body was slender and elongated, and there were

strong limbs and feet, which enabled the animal to walk on land.
Size: Mesozoic crocodiles are generally 2–3m (6½–9¾ft) long. In Texas, USA, a crocodile skull over 2m (6½ft) long has been found.
Occurrence: Remains of crocodiles are not uncommon in marine and brackish-water sediments of Triassic, Jurassic and Cretaceous age, worldwide.
Comments: Crocodiles are close relatives of the dinosaurs, evolving during the late Triassic period. They flourished in the Jurassic period, and there were more genera during Cretaceous time than there are today. Many survived the mass extinction at the end of the Cretaceous period, during which the dinosaurs and numerous other creatures died out. One of the first Mesozoic crocodiles to be described scientifically in the 1930s was found by Navajo Indians in Arizona, USA.

ARCHAEOPTERYX

This bird-like fossil has a long, narrow nose with small teeth in its jaws. Its neck is slim and very bird-like, but the tail is reptilian, and there are clawed fingers in the wings (see image on p.218). The bones lack the hollow air cavity structures that are characteristic of bird skeletons. There are large eye sockets in the skull, and the brain would have been relatively large. The main bird-like feature, which is preserved in all but one of the known specimens, is the outline of feathers around the wings and tail.
Size: The skull of *Archaeopteryx* is about the same size as that of a pigeon, but overall the body is somewhat larger than a pigeon's.
Occurrence: This rare fossil has only been found in strata of Jurassic age near Solnhofen, southern Germany.
Comments: The example illustrated is a cast of the famous

VERTEBRATE FOSSILS

specimen housed in the Museum of Natural History in Berlin.
There are very few examples of this important fossil species. Their
discovery has at times caused controversy, and there is still much
debate surrounding them. The first specimen was found in 1861,
and is now in the British Museum (Natural History) in London. In
1877 another, better preserved individual, including a skull, was
found, and the third example was not discovered until 1951. This
was not initially recognized as *Archaeopteryx*, as it was without
feathers. It was named *Compsognathus*, and was believed to be a
small dinosaur. In 1956, a headless body was found, and two more
have since turned up in collections, labelled as small dinosaurs.
Even though *Archaeopteryx* has some strange features, it is a
definite link between reptiles and birds.

MAMMUTHUS

The illustration is of a cheek tooth from this large mammal. Its surface
is well adapted for grinding vegetation, and has a series of strong
ridges. This is one of the most common fossils from *Mammuthus*.
Size: The tooth is 250mm (10in) long. The whole animal grew to
around 2.8m (9ft) high.
Occurrence: In rocks of Pleistocene age in Europe, Asia and North
America.
Comments: The remains of mammals from Cenozoic rocks are not
uncommon. Mammoth fossils, including teeth and disarticulated
bones, are frequently found in river deposits such as sand and
gravel. Indeed, these fossils are often discovered during the
commercial exploitation of such material. *Mammuthus* is probably

the best documented ice-age mammal, large numbers of bones and teeth having been preserved in the frozen tundra of Alaska and

northern Russia. In Siberia virtually complete mammoths began to be discovered in the 18th and 19th centuries, and these were frequently plundered for their ivory. The fossils were so complete that even stomach contents could be studied. *Mammuthus* became extinct only around 10,000 years ago in North America and 12,000 years ago in Europe. They were hunted by early humans, and depicted in carvings and cave paintings.

CROCUTA

This jaw bone is from a cave hyena called *Crocuta*. These ice-age mammals were similar to modern hyenas, but were more solidly built and slightly larger. This was probably in response to the

VERTEBRATE FOSSILS

rigours of the cold, Pleistocene climate. The jaws were strong, with good muscles and teeth capable of crushing the large bones of mammoths and rhinos. Carrion may have been their main food, and they were probably nomadic, following herds of herbivores across the tundra landscape.

Size: This jaw is 150mm (6in) long.

Occurrence: In cave deposits, gravels and other sediments of Pleistocene age, worldwide.

Comments: The genus became extinct around the same time as the cave bear, when the last glacial advance was at its height.

URSUS

This specimen is a tooth from a cave bear (*Ursus*). These large mammals lived on the glacial margins during the last ice age. They hibernated in caves during the colder season, and probably lived there most of the year in small groups. Their remains are often found in large numbers in cave deposits. The molar teeth are

frequently worn down, suggesting a vegetarian diet, at least during the warm season.

Size: The tooth illustrated is 30mm (1⅛in) long. This species was not as large as the brown bear, and its skull is very different, being high and domed.

Occurrence: In Pleistocene cave deposits in Europe and North America. The specimen is from North America.

Comments: Cave bears were hunted by man, but this in no way threatened their total population. The increasing cold of the last glacial advance depleted their food supply, and they became extinct midway through the final glaciation of the Pleistocene.

BALAENA

This rather strange-looking fossil is the ear bone from the whale, *Balaena*. It has a rounded, almost mollusc-shell shape. Whales evolved during the Cenozoic era, after the decline of the great marine reptiles that had been predators in the Jurassic and Cretaceous oceans. Some of the smaller cetaceans, such as dolphins and porpoises, bear a striking similarity to the ichthyosaurs.

Size: The ear bone illustrated is 50mm (2in) long.
Occurrence: In marine rocks of Cenozoic age, worldwide.
Comments: The modern whales evolved from the mid-Cenozoic. Some earlier genera such as *Basilosaurus*, which lived during the Eocene epoch, grew to over 20m (65ft) in length.

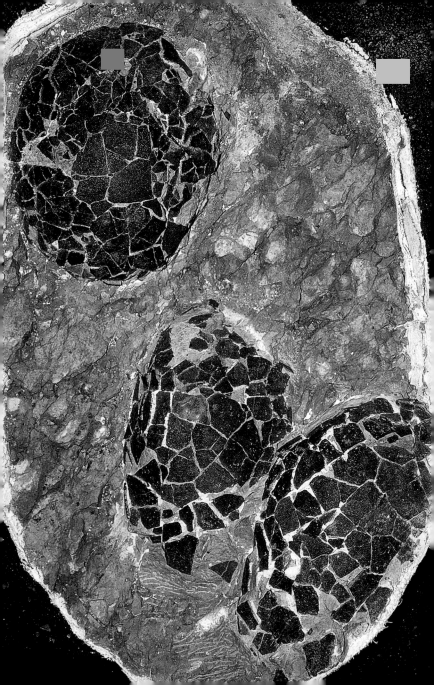

TRACE FOSSILS

Trace fossils are the burrows, tracks and trails, excrement and footprints that animals have made and which are preserved in rocks. Many organisms leave such evidence of their way of life. The scientific name ichnofossil (Greek, *ichnos*, a track) is used for trace fossils, and their study helps palaeontologists to discover much about the life of the animals that left such traces. In some cases it is only the trace that is left. A soft-bodied worm may never be preserved, but its burrows, especially if they are infilled with sediment, can readily become fossilized. Many other invertebrate organisms burrow into sediment. Bivalve molluscs such as *Pholadomya*, the brachiopod *Lingula*, and some arthropods all make burrows in seabed mud or sand. Tracks and trails on the surface of sediment are made by gastropods, trilobites and other arthropods. One of the problems is that even by analogy with modern animals' tracks and burrows, it is often very difficult to determine what made a trace fossil. Such fossils are given scientific names of their own, not the name of the animal that made them.

For a trace left by an organism to be fossilized, it needs to be infilled with sediment soon after formation. A burrow, unless it is lined with calcite or similar hardening material, may collapse, but if mud or sand washes in, it may be preserved in three dimensions. Tracks, trails and footprints must similarly have a new layer of sediment deposited on them before they can be removed by erosion. These trace fossils may then be discovered as bedding planes are split open, with a mould, the actual track or footprint, on one surface, and the cast, or infilling, on the other.

Some of the best known trace fossils are the footprints of dinosaurs. These are found in many parts of the world, and may consist of solitary impressions or of whole trackways containing many prints. Much can be learned about a dinosaur from its footprints, including its size, weight and speed of movement. Taking modern animals as a starting point, a formula that relates velocity to the

OPPOSITE: Dinosaur eggs. Much information has come to light in recent years about dinosaur 'nests' and young. Some species seem to have nested in colonies, and eggs containing embryos have been found in the USA. The illustration opposite shows eggs from Cretaceous rock in Mongolia.

length of the stride has been devised. Using this formula it has been suggested that sauropods found in Texas, USA, moved at 3.6km/h (2½mph), and that small herbivores fossilized in Australia ran across wet mud at 15km/h (9½mph).

CRUZIANA
The impressions preserved on this rock surface are the distinctive trails believed to have been made by trilobites. They consist of a series of roughly parallel furrows and raised ridges.
Size: The specimen illustrated is 140mm (5⅝in) long.
Occurrence: *Cruziana* has been found in Palaeozoic and Mesozoic rocks, worldwide. The specimen illustrated is from Ordovician strata near Rennes, France.

Comments: There has been much argument about *Cruziana*, and because very similar trace fossils have been found in rocks far younger than those that contain trilobites, it is thought that this fossil could be made by other creatures such as isopods (pillbug-like organisms). Sometimes another lobe-shaped trace fossil called *Rusophycus* is found with *Cruziana*. This may be the impression left in soft, seabed mud where a trilobite or other organism rested.

THALASSINOIDES

These dark-coloured markings are infilled burrows, probably made by a marine crustacean. When bedding planes are split apart, trace fossils are found that consist of a raised cast on one surface (as here) and a negative mould on the other surface. This fossil is made up of branching burrows, often 'Y'-shaped in structure.

Size: The specimen shown is 150mm (6in) across the field of view.

Occurrence: *Thalassinoides* occurs in rocks of Jurassic age, world-wide. The specimen is from North Yorkshire, UK.

Comments: The marine arthropod *Glyphea* (see pp.134–135) has been found associated with these trace fossils and may have made them. *Thalassinoides* burrows were just below the sediment surface and parallel to it, not vertically into the mud.

LITHOPHAGA BURROWS AND POLYCHAETE WORM BURROWS

Two distinct trace fossils occur in this specimen. The pale, round-ed markings (top) are the burrows made by the bivalve mollusc, *Lithophaga*. This creature could bore into the hard limestone (the dark-coloured rock) of the Jurassic seabed. The thin, tube-shaped burrows were made by polychaete worms.

Size: The rounded *Lithophaga* burrows are 10mm (⅜in) across.

Occurrence: In strata of Jurassic age, worldwide. The specimen is from the Mendip Hills, Somerset, UK.

TRACE FOSSILS

Comments: This specimen is of interest because it shows rocks of two very different ages. The dark rock in the lower part of the specimen is Carboniferous limestone, while the paler material infilling

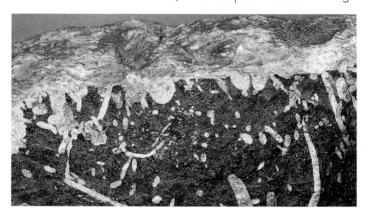

the burrows is limestone of Jurassic age. The surface into which the burrows have been made is an unconformity and represents a 'time gap' of well over 150 million years. During this time rocks would have been deposited and then eroded, so that no actual record of geological events is left where the unconformity occurs.

ROTULARIA

These trace fossils could be mistaken for gastropod shells, but they are in fact worm burrows. They have a spiral, calcareous structure, and occur weathered out of the sediment in which they were formed.
Size: These fossils are 15mm (⅜in) across.

Occurrence: In Cenozoic strata, worldwide. The examples shown are from Eocene rocks in Sussex, UK.

Comments: The worms that made these burrows are related to those that created the trace fossils shown on p.226. They are marine worms, often referred to as scale worms, bristle worms and ragworms; today they live in shallow marine conditions. *Rotularia* survives as a trace fossil because the worm strengthened its burrow with calcium carbonate.

DINOSAUR FOOTPRINT

This three-toed footprint shows the marks of slender toes, two possibly longer than the third. No remains of the dinosaur itself have been found. It was preserved by the infilling of the original print, and when the bedding planes were split the original impression was revealed. Research has shown that the same animal may produce prints of different shapes, depending on whether it stepped in very wet or dry mud, so different prints can belong to the same species.

Size. This print is 100mm (4in) long.

Occurrence: In Jurassic strata in North Yorkshire, UK. Dinosaur footprints are well known in Mesozoic rocks in many parts of the world.

Comments: This footprint is associated with many others and with trackways consisting of numerous aligned prints. Different prints made by a variety of dinosaurs indicate that the environment where they are found was a very suitable habitat. This was a river flood-

TRACE FOSSILS

plain, with swamps and luxuriant vegetation. Even though remains of these dinosaurs have not been found, it is possible, from their footprints, to estimate their size and structure by relating them to modern creatures.

COPROLITE

Coprolites are fossil droppings, left in this example by a marine turtle. The brownish colouring is produced by a covering of iron oxide.
Size: This fossil is 30mm (1⅛in) long, but much larger examples have been found. Fecal pellets are smaller, and are left by fishes and invertebrates.

Occurrence: The coprolite illustrated is from Eocene rocks in the USA, but coprolites and fecal pellets are also known worldwide from rocks of Palaeozoic to Recent age.
Comments: These fossils can give valuable information about the diet and digestive system of the creature that produced them. Some contain the remains of fish scales, insect legs or carapaces, vertebrate bones, mollusc shells or plant fragments.

SKOLITHUS

The thin, pale markings on this cliff face are the infilled burrows of marine worms. The rock in which they occur is a pinkish quartzite, and the paler quartzite filling the burrows makes them very apparent. Also shown is a hand specimen showing the top surface of a bedding plane.
Size: The individual burrows are about 10mm (⅜in) in width.
Occurrence: Burrows such as these are common trace fossils in rocks of many ages, worldwide. The example is from rocks of

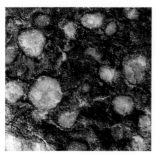

Cambrian age in Sutherland, Scotland, UK.

Comments: The soft-bodied marine worms that made these burrows would have had virtually no chance of becoming fossilized. Today, intertidal mud flats are often full of worms, and their burrows can be located by casts left above them on the mud at low tide. The sand in which these burrows were originally made was probably formed in shallow marine conditions on the margins of a continental shelf.

SKOLICIA

This trace fossil consists of slender, curving ridges, some with a notable sharp crest. There are faint 'ribs' running down the slopes from the crest.

Size: The whole specimen is 250mm (10in) across.

Occurrence: *Skolicia*-type trace fossils are known from rocks ranging in age from Palaeozoic to Recent. The example is from the Carboniferous of Yorkshire, UK.

Comments: *Skolicia* is a grazing trail produced by a marine gastropod. This sea snail would have left a sinuous hollow in the seabed, which was infilled with mud and so preserved.

TRACE FOSSILS

GLOSSARY

adductor muscles Sets of muscles used to close a brachiopod shell.

amber An organically formed mineral, made of hardened tree resin.

Ambulacra (sing. ambulacrum) Rows of plates making up part of an echinoid test. In the regular echinoids, they run in bands around the test, but in irregular forms they may be stunted or petal-shaped.

articulata The class of brachiopods that are able to open their valves slightly.

atrophied Shortened or stunted.

bedding Layering in sedimentary rocks, strata.

benthonic On the seabed.

birfurcate To split into two parts, as in the ribs of ammonites, which may divide.

bilateral Symmetry with two similar or identical halves.

byssus Thread-like material with which certain bivalve molluscs attach themselves.

calcite A mineral made of calcium carbonate. Many organisms secrete this mineral to form their shells and skeletons. It is also a major constituent of limestone.

calice A hollow in the top of a coral in which the coral polyp lived.

carapace The exoskeleton of an arthropod.

cast The replica of an organism made by the infilling of an impression it left in sediment.

chalk A very fine-grained limestone made of the calcite shells of microscopic marine organisms.

chert A hard rock made from silica. Often it occurs as nodules or discrete masses in limestone.

chitin The tough horny material present in the carapaces of arthropods. It also occurs in many other organisms.

cleavage In rocks, this refers to the parallel planes in slate, produced by an alignment of minerals during metamorphism.

corallite An individual coral structure. These may be joined in a colony.

crust The solid, rocky, outer-most layer of the Earth. In the ocean basins it is relatively thin (8km, 5 miles thick), but under the continental regions much thicker (80km, 50 miles thick).

dorsal Referring to the 'back' of an organism, and opposite of ventral.

era A very long period of geological time, further subdivided into periods.

erosion The removal and breakdown of the Earth's surface by processes involving movement, including rivers, glaciers and the sea.

evolute Describes the coiling of a cephalopod shell when the whorls overlap only slightly.

exoskeleton An external skeleton. The carapace of an arthropod is its exoskeleton.

flint A type of chert made of microcrystalline silica. Usually it occurs as rows of discrete nodules in chalk.

Foraminifera Single-celled marine organisms classified among the Protozoa.

Gondwanaland The gigantic, ancient continent of the Palaeozoic and Mesozoic eras that split up to form Australia, India, Antarctica, Africa and South America.

growth lines Lines on a shell that mark a former position of the shell margin.

hematite A mineral composed of iron oxide. It is usually reddish in colour and can replace original material during fossilization.

hinge line The margin of a brachiopod or bivalve mollusc shell where the mechanism for opening the valves is situated.

ichnology The study of fossil footprints.

interglacial The time between main advances of ice during an ice age.

invertebrate An animal with-out an internal skeleton.

involute Describes the coiling of a cephalopod shell in which the whorls overlap a great deal.

limestone A type of sedimentary rock composed mainly of calcium carbonate. It may also contain lesser amounts of clay, quartz and other minerals, and is usually fossiliferous.

lycopods A group of primitive plants, also called clubmosses.

mica A group of silicate minerals. They are soft and flaky, and form initially in igneous and metamorphic rocks.

Monoplacophora A primitive class of molluscs with a single valve.

mould An impression left in soft sediment by an organism. This may be filled in to produce a cast.

nodule A rounded or irregularly shaped mass of rock, usually only a few centimetres across, in which fossils often occur. Nodules are found in many sedimentary rocks, especially shale and clay.

oolith A small, rounded sediment grain, usually made of calcite. Ooliths have a concentric, layered structure and form oolitic limestone.

palaeogeography The geography of the Earth in the distant past.

pentameral Based on five, as in the pentameral symmetry of a regular echinoid test.

period One of the main divisions of geological time. Periods are grouped together into eras.

permeable Allowing water, or other fluids, to pass through along cracks and fractures.

phylum A group of organisms with broadly similar characteristics. This is further subdivided into smaller groups including genus and species.

planktonic Very close to the surface of the sea.

polyp The soft-bodied marine animal that secretes a coral.

porous With small holes through which fluids can penetrate.

pyrite A mineral formed of iron sulphide. Nodules in sedimentary rocks are often composed of pyrite, as are fossils.

quartz A very common oxide mineral, composed of silicon dioxide. It may replace original material during fossilization.

reef A mound of sediment, the top of which is close to the sea's surface.

septum (pl. septa) an internal division in a mollusc shell or a coral.

shale A fine-grained, sedimentary rock, originally mud.

stratum (pl. strata) A bed or layer of sedimentary rock.

system The rocks formed during a period of geological time.

test An outer shell, especially of an echinoid.

thorax The central section of the body of some organisms, between head and abdomen.

umbilicus The very middle of a coiled shell.

umbo The pointed or beak-shaped part of a brachiopod or bivalve mollusc shell.

ventral Referring to the underneath surface of an organism, the opposite of dorsal.

whorl A single coil of a shell, as in some cephalopods and gastropods.

zone A short, precise unit of geological time. Periods are made up of many zones, which may each represent less than one million years.

FURTHER READING

The following list of recommended titles is by no means exhaustive, but will help the reader explore the material and ideas in this book.

Barthel, K.W., N.M.H. Swinburn and Morris S. Conway, *Solnhofen, a Study in Mesozoic Palaeontology*, Cambridge University Press, 1990.

Benton, M.J., *Vertebrate Palaeontology*, Chapman Hall, London, 1995.

British Museum, Natural History, *British Palaeozoic Fossils*, British Museum, London, 1995.

British Museum, Natural History, *British Mesozoic Fossils*, British Museum, London, 1995.

British Museum, Natural History, *British Cenozoic Fossils*, British Museum, London, 1995.

Bromley, R., *Trace Fossils*, Chapman Hall, London, 1995.

Donovan, S.K., *The Process of Fossilisation*, Belhaven Press, London, 1990

Fastovsky, D. & D. Weishampel, *The Evolution and Extinction of the Dinosaurs*, Cambridge University Press, 2005.

Gould, S.J., *Wonderful Life, The Burgess Shale and the Nature of History*, Norton, New York, 1989.

Gradstein, F., J. Ogg and A. Smith, *A Geologic Time Scale*, Cambridge, 2005.

Kenrick, P. and P. Davis, *Fossil Plants*, Natural History Museum, London, 2004.

Moore, M.C., *Treatise on Invertebrate Palaeontology*, University of Kansas, 1953 onwards.

Morton, J.E., *Molluscs*, Hutchinson, London, 1967.

Murray, J.W., *Atlas of Invertebrate Macrofossils*, Longman, Harlow, 1985.

Norman. D., *Illustrated Encyclopedia of Dinosaurs*, Salamander, London, 1985.

Pellant, C., *Rocks, Minerals and Fossils of the World*, Pan Books, London, 1990.

Rudwick, M.J.S., *Living and Fossil Brachiopods*, Hutchinson, London, 1970.

Walker, C., and D. Ward, *Smithsonian Handbooks, Fossils*, Dorling Kindersley, London, 2001.

Whitten, D.G.A., & J.R.V. Brooks, *The Penguin Dictionary of Geology*, London, 1990

WEBSITES

Much information can be found on the internet. By using a search engine and entering the name of a fossil or locality, it is usually possible to find details. Some particularly useful websites are listed below, but there are many others.

www.discoveringfossils.co.uk
www.ukfossils.co.uk
www.nhm.ac.uk/interactive/urml (The Natural History Museum, London, UK)
www.geolsoc.org (The Geological Society of London, UK)
www.sedgwickmuseum.org (The Sedgwick Museum, Cambridge, UK)
www.nationmaster.com/encyclopedia/list-of-u.s.-state-fossils
www.si.edu (The Smithsonian Museum, Washington, DC, USA, which has one of the world's finest fossil collections)
www.fieldmuseum.org (The Field Museum, Connecticut, USA, has the most complete *Tyrannosaurus rex* skeleton.)

ACKNOWLEDGEMENTS

A number of people helped us during the planning, photography and writing of this book. We must first thank Jo Hemmings for originally suggesting the title to us, and Steffanie Brown and James Parry for their editorial work. Henry Russell cast his very thorough eye over our text and captions and made many useful suggestions., both about the book and the summer's test matches. We are grateful also to Sid Weatherill (Hildoceras) of Whitby, who allowed us free access to their fossil collections for photography. Martin Rigby and his wife Mary of Fossils Direct also made us most welcome and allowed us to photograph specimens from what must be one of the best private fossil collections in Britain.

INDEX